Reclaiming
Church

Reclaiming Church

Christopher Brearley

Sovereign World

Sovereign World Ltd
PO Box 784
Ellel
Lancaster LA1 9DA
England

www.sovereignworld.com

ISBN: 978-1-85240-536-6

The publishers aim to produce books which will help to extend and build up the Kingdom of God. We do not necessarily agree with every view expressed by the authors, or with every interpretation of Scripture expressed. We expect readers to make their own judgment in the light of their understanding of God's Word and in an attitude of Christian love and fellowship.

Cover design by ThirteenFour Design
Typeset by documen, www.documen.co.uk
Printed in the United Kingdom

Contents

	Introduction	7
Chapter 1	A Supernatural Church	9
Chapter 2	A Shared Ministry	25
Chapter 3	New Testament Patterns for Evangelism and Church Planting	45
Chapter 4	Disagreements, Divisions, and Discipline	65
Chapter 5	House Meetings and Cell Groups	87
Chapter 6	Reactions to the Gospel	105
	About the Author	126

Introduction

How do you view the future? Is it with fear and foreboding, or with hope and great expectation? The Greek philosopher Aristotle (384–322 BC) said, "When I look at the younger generation, I despair at the future of civilization." That echoes what some are saying now. Although the conditions of life vary tremendously from one generation to the next, human nature does not change. A recurring feature of history is the depression and despondency that people feel because of the problems caused by human beings of all age groups. What has been will be again; what has been done will be done again. Is there any hope anywhere? Or are we all facing ruin and despair?

Luke, who wrote the book of Acts under the inspiration of the Holy Spirit, reveals that the early years of the Christian Church were not all rapture and righteousness. There were serious faults and imperfections that needed to be corrected. Irrespective of this, it was a time of tremendous blessing and thousands came to know Jesus Christ as their Lord and Savior. The outpouring of the Holy Spirit brought about a radical change. If the Church is to reclaim her former glory she must return to the basics as outlined in Scripture.

Today many churches, especially in North America and Europe, are plagued by liberalism and proclaim a caricature of the true gospel of salvation. At the other extreme are militant traditionalists who find it difficult, even impossible, not to be separatists. As a result, the principles of first-century churches have often become lost for a wide range of reasons. It should be no surprise that overall the Church is in a state of sharp decline. What possibility is there for revival in such an irreligious age as our own? We can't produce a revival, but I believe we can facilitate it. How? The answer is by persistent, fervent prayer, by personal revival (Luke 11:13), and by boldly proclaiming the true gospel at every opportunity.

The way to encourage someone in the Christian life is not to tell him or her that it is going to be easy. Quite the contrary, it is a battle against evil supernatural forces. Even so, every believer is meant to be an active soldier of Christ Jesus and will therefore require the full armor of God. Christians must constantly be aware of their utter dependence upon the infinite supernatural power of God if they are to survive the battle.

My purpose in writing this book is to examine the important characteristics of the New Testament Church and then to see how they should be applied to the twenty-first century. Are the gifts of the Spirit for today? According to the New Testament, the Holy Spirit is the One sent to us by the Father, in answer to the request of the Son, to be our Helper for ever (John 14:15–31).

Our need of the Spirit's power to achieve what we could never accomplish on our own has not changed. God has not changed. The Bible has not changed. Our need of salvation has not changed. Our call to go and make disciples of all nations, baptizing them in the name of the Father and of the Son and of the Holy Spirit, has not changed. The King of kings is still upon the throne of heaven and will always be there.

Christopher Brearley

CHAPTER 1

A Supernatural Church

A major characteristic of the early Church, in spite of its many failures, is that it was mightily blessed by the presence of the Holy Spirit. It was a Spirit-guided community and that was the source of its power. Then, and now, people are transformed as the Spirit enters their lives. There can be no life without the Life Giver. No vision or strategies will bear any worthwhile fruit without the power of the Holy Spirit.

> Unless the LORD builds the house,
> its builders labor in vain.

> (Psalm 127:1)

The Holy Spirit is the infinite power of God, and without that power nothing of any lasting value can ever be accomplished. Accordingly, there is an urgent need to pray for an outpouring of God's Spirit upon His Church and its witness today!

To speak of the "coming" of the Holy Spirit at Pentecost can be misleading. It could wrongly imply that the Holy Spirit originated then, whereas He exists eternally in perfect union with the Father and the Son. The book of Acts makes that abundantly clear. For instance, the Holy Spirit spoke long ago through the mouth of David (Acts 1:16); the Spirit spoke through Isaiah (Acts 28:25); Stephen emphatically accuses the Jews of sinning against the Spirit all through their history (Acts 7:51).

Although the Spirit is present in every age, something extraordinary happened at Pentecost.

> All of them were filled with the Holy Spirit and began to speak in other tongues as the Spirit enabled them.
>
> (Acts 2:4)

The Holy Spirit came on the Day of Pentecost and He has never abandoned the Church. How then can we obtain the fullness of God's power so as to be fully equipped for every good thing God wants us to do? The answer is that He gives it to those who seek Him (Acts 4:31) and obey Him (Acts 5:32). This giving of the power of His Spirit is not for our personal satisfaction but always for God's glory alone.

To be filled with the Spirit is a recurring feature within the New Testament. Christians were "filled" with power for service (Acts 2:4; 4:8, 31; 9:17; 13:9). Some of those who had previously been blessed at Pentecost received further outpourings so that they could face new challenges and again be able to speak the Word of God with boldness.

To avoid confusion we must differentiate between Spirit "filling," as previously described, and Spirit "baptism." The latter occurs only once in a person's life, for it is the spiritual work of God whereby one becomes part of the Body of Christ (1 Corinthians 12:13). That is applicable to all Christians because they are "in Christ."

Luke provides us with a vivid picture of the first Spirit-filled Christian community following the sudden blessing of Pentecost. Many supernatural happenings occurred at this momentous time and thousands were added to the Church. An outpouring of the Holy Spirit brought about a radical

change. Sadly, few churches today can claim to be growing at such a phenomenal rate through conversions. Quite
the contrary, most churches are struggling and some are
unlikely to survive unless they urgently test what they do
in the light of Scripture, and adapt. So what did the early
Christians do that we would be wise to emulate?

> They devoted themselves to the apostles' teaching and to the
> fellowship, to the breaking of bread and to prayer. Everyone
> was filled with awe, and many wonders and miraculous signs
> were done by the apostles. All the believers were together and
> had everything in common. Selling their possessions and goods,
> they gave to anyone as he had need. Every day they continued
> to meet together in the temple courts. They broke bread in
> their homes and ate together with glad and sincere hearts, prais-
> ing God and enjoying the favor of all the people. And the Lord
> added to their number daily those who were being saved.
>
> (Acts 2:42–47)

From the above, we see that the early Church had eight outstanding characteristics:

1. It was a learning church

An obvious evidence of the Spirit's presence is that the
Church dedicated itself to the authoritative teaching of
the apostles which was authenticated by many wonders
and miraculous signs. These new converts were eager to
receive instruction and they persevered to learn all that they
could. They rightly recognized the apostles, whom Jesus
had personally trained during His three-year ministry, as the
teachers of the Church.

Is this applicable to ourselves and our churches? Certainly, there are no apostles today who have authority

comparable to the Twelve, but in the early Church there were teachers, other than the apostles, whose teaching would be judged in comparison to what the apostles taught. Likewise, all teachers today must be judged according to their faithfulness to the apostolic teaching found in the New Testament. This is to be steadfastly adhered to throughout all generations so as to avoid the contamination of divine truth. Christians are to continually devote themselves to learning about what God has done for them and how they might live in a right relationship with Him. This is fundamental to the growth of all Christians.

How this is achieved will vary from one individual to another. It is not always desirable to restrict ourselves to specific methods of teaching. Although Sunday sermons and Bible studies during the week are the most common sources, they are not sacrosanct. We might consider small-group discussion or a sermon followed by an opportunity for questions. Whatever forms of teaching are adopted, the elders must play a central role and ensure that those for whom they are responsible grow in their faith.

My own experience suggests that many sermons are far too long. Some preachers frequently fail to realize that whilst they may be enjoying themselves in the pulpit, their hearers in the pew are not. Any preachers who aimlessly wander from one anecdote to another would be wise to concentrate on the points that really matter and also learn to stop speaking when their audience stops listening. The aim should always be for quality rather than quantity. Some gifted preachers can achieve both.

People who suggest that acquiring knowledge and being filled with the Holy Spirit are incompatible make a serious error. The Holy Spirit is "the Spirit of truth" and so directs us to study and submit to the Word of God that constitutes our infallible rule of faith and practice. God wants His people to be continual learners who discover something new every day. It is always a sign of a spiritual decline when the yearning to know Him better diminishes. A Spirit-filled church is distinguished by its insatiable appetite to learn and obey what Jesus and His apostles taught.

2. It was a church that enjoyed fellowship

Christians who love the Lord and so love each other will naturally desire to meet together as often as possible. They are not happy to be apart. That is why Scripture says,

> They devoted themselves ... to the fellowship.
>
> (Acts 2:42)

There was a constant sense of togetherness because of their newfound life in Christ. The Church consists of brothers and sisters who devote themselves to each other because of mutual love.

> Every day they continued to meet together in the temple courts. They broke bread in their homes and ate together with glad and sincere hearts.
>
> (Acts 2:46)

Undoubtedly, this was a powerful witness to the risen Christ, for anyone could see how the believers loved one another in true fellowship.

The breaking of bread is surely a reference to the Lord's Supper, or Holy Communion, though most likely this also included a fellowship meal, for hospitality among the early Christians was vital to their spiritual growth. Clearly, they enjoyed their fellowship, whether it was in a large formal group in the temple courts, or in small informal groups in each other's homes. Both are important in the life of the Church and therefore should be reflected in meaningful ways in our fellowship (see chapter 5).

So often today, Christians meet only once on a Sunday and consequently miss the necessary opportunities to interact on a regular basis and be part of a family gathering. Unquestionably, Christians who love the Lord should instinctively love each other and desire to meet together whenever possible. To me, it is clear that most churches need to recapture more of a sense of close community if they are to succeed in sharing themselves and their Lord with others.

Admittedly, the period immediately following Pentecost was unusual and it would be wrong to generalize from such special circumstances. It was still festival time, which meant that many people were on holiday and so could meet daily to study the apostles' teaching. Probably in most instances, this would not continue once they were dispersed far and wide. Also, to keep everyone together during this vital formative period it was necessary for Christians to merge their resources. That is why the believers had "everything in common."

Although the early Church is not an exact model for today, it nevertheless remains true that Christians should meet frequently, both formally and informally, as a community. They should also give sacrificially out of a grateful heart to those in genuine need.

3. It was a caring church

The early Christians had an intense attitude of responsibility and willingly made great sacrifices for each other. Whenever there was a genuine need, those who were able gave help. This is to put into practice what John writes about in his letter:

If anyone has material possessions and sees his brother in need but has no pity on him, how can the love of God be in him? Dear children, let us not love with words or tongue but with actions and in truth.

(1 John 3:17–18)

Actions always speak louder than words.

How does this apply to the Church today? Could there not be a tendency for some Christians to abuse such a system? Certainly Paul thought so, and makes his views about idleness abundantly clear when writing to the Thessalonians.

If a man will not work, he shall not eat.

(2 Thessalonians 3:10)

He had no sympathy whatever with the attitude of people who were unwilling to work, but he was always willing to help those who were genuinely in need.

Should Christians follow the example set by the Essene leaders of the Qumran community and renounce the right to private ownership, establish a common fund, and share the proceeds? Doubtless we must be careful to avoid extreme interpretations. We cannot say it is a mistake to claim that our possessions are not our own. Nor can we pretend that such actions of generosity are obligatory and that all our property must be sold and the proceeds shared with others through a scheme of common ownership. That is a Marxist, not a Christian, belief.

Spirituality should be equated with sacrificial giving and not poverty or wealth. The general idea is not that the rich must sell all their property and so become poor. Rather, within the New Testament, sharing one's wealth was a spontaneous, voluntary gesture made only at intervals when funds were urgently required. An example

of an exception to this was the case of the rich young man
whom Jesus told,

> Go, sell everything you have and give to the poor, and you will
> have treasure in heaven.
>
> (Mark 10:21)

This was an exception because in this instance he loved
earthly possessions and so it was the necessary and only
cure for his greed.

God gives us things which we do not deserve. Consequently, we should be grateful and show it by our generosity. It
is a fact that our Christian generosity to others is related to our
gratitude towards God whom we can never repay. This is well
illustrated by the life of the rich and influential Zacchaeus, who
said to Jesus,

> "Look, Lord! Here and now I give half of my possessions to the
> poor, and if I have cheated anybody out of anything, I will pay
> back four times the amount."
>
> (Luke 19:8)

The Law (Exodus 22:4, 7, 9) stated that double restitution
was required in some instances for what had been unjustly
obtained. Zacchaeus, however, has promised not to restore
double but fourfold to anyone whom he might have over-
charged. Although such actions do not earn salvation, they
are a sign of a grateful heart.

4. It was a praying church

Throughout the book of Acts we see that the early Christians
realized that they could not succeed by their own strength
and moreover that they did not need to. Acts 4 reveals that

during a time of great danger they prayed for boldness in preaching, and also asked that their words would be authenticated by miraculous works of healing, and similar signs and wonders, through the Name of Jesus.

In the above instance, the assurance of divine favor was fulfilled as they prayed. The building where they met shook and they were filled with the Holy Spirit and thus enabled to preach God's Word without fear.

Likewise, Acts 12 illustrates people's inability to withstand God's power. Herod Agrippa I, grandson of Herod the Great, had Peter arrested and imprisoned during the Passover celebration so as to ingratiate himself with the Jews. But while Peter was in prison, the Church prayed earnestly for him, and to their amazement he miraculously escaped. Perhaps they had been praying for Peter's acquittal at his trial, which would explain their surprise and also why they did not believe the maid, Rhoda, when she said,

Peter is at the door!

(Acts 12:14)

God had encouraged them by giving them not what they had asked for, but something much better. No doubt those who attended the prayer meeting that night would have been comforted and strengthened, for earnest prayer changes people and situations.

It would be wrong to assume that the early believers prayed only in times of difficulty. Prayer was their first response rather than a last resort. When the seven officebearers were appointed in Acts 6, the apostles presented them in prayer to God. In Acts 13 we see that, after fasting and prayer, Paul and Barnabas were sent out on their first missionary journey. Then in Acts 20 there was prayer when Paul said farewell to the Ephesian elders.

The early Church devoted itself to prayer because Christians realized their complete dependence upon God. This raises an important question. Why is it that so often the worst attended meeting of churches today is the prayer meeting? Is prayer considered to be unimportant? Or are these meetings so badly organized that only a few want to attend? Certainly, some churches need to urgently consider their prayer life in the light of Biblical teaching. Any church that prays half-heartedly for God's intervention and tremendous blessing is unlikely to see a radical transformation. Only by realizing our sense of weakness and our utter dependence upon God can we pray rightly.

Generally, intense prayer precedes revival. However, God is sovereign in the manner, time, and range of the manifestations of His power and is never limited to a stereotype. We cannot pressurize Him into acting on our behalf, but instead we are dependent upon His love and mercy and the assurance that He will provide for all our needs.

Prayer is the essential communication between ourselves and God through which we can develop an intimate relationship. It is primarily an act of worship through which we praise our Almighty God. As we come to accept the necessity of prayer in our lives, it becomes clear why Jesus taught His disciples to pray (Matthew 6:9–13). He teaches them to avoid meaningless verbosity and through an economy of words reveals a framework upon which we can build. Effective prayer includes the elements of adoration, confession, and dedication, as well as requests.

Prayer will sometimes be expressed silently, sometimes audibly; very often privately but also corporately. It will increasingly become a disposition of our character as we grow to be more like Jesus. The earnest, specific prayer of a righteous person has great power and this should be no surprise (James 5:16). In places such as Korea and China, the common ingredient in the explosive growth of the Church consistently emerges as prayer. The early Church devoted itself to prayer and many people were won for Christ.

5. It was a worshipping church

The noun "worship" is a contraction of "worthship." Therefore, to worship God is to acknowledge His worth and worthiness. Primarily, the Church is a worshipping, praying community that gives ceaseless praise and thanks to God, and rejoices because of all that He has done and all that He will do.

Jesus reminds us that the first and greatest commandment is:

> Love the Lord your God with all your heart and with all your soul and with all your mind.
>
> (Matthew 22:37)

This is to be our number one priority. Love for our neighbor is the second commandment, which implies that evangelism, although essential, is secondary to the worship of God.

Christians may worship in many different ways providing that it is sincere and scriptural. Some will prefer a formal and dignified service whilst others, especially the younger generation, prefer informal, freer meetings. Both can be pleasing in God's sight, providing that the former does not become a ritualistic formality and the latter a form of spiritual entertainment. The vital test is whether one's worship is wholehearted. Does it glorify God in spirit and truth? If it does, then we must respect each other's preferences for worship so as to maintain a healthy balance.

6. It was a joyful church

To the Christian, worship is a joy. It will be so in heaven; it can be so now on earth. A miserable Christian is a paradox and certainly no recommendation for the Christian faith. Nevertheless there are those who give the impression that they meet out of a sense of duty rather than a sense of delight, unlike the early believers who exhibited exuberant joy.

All Christians have a good reason to be filled with an inexpressible and glorious joy, because through the work of Christ they obtain salvation. Furthermore, joy is a fruit of the Holy Spirit (Galatians 5:22). Those who are filled with the Spirit will be joyful and look far beyond the problems of daily life to their future glory. That is why the early Christians, despite many trials, could thank and praise God. When Paul and Silas were severely flogged and thrown into prison, they prayed and sang hymns, thus revealing the triumph of faith over affliction. It's no wonder "the other prisoners were listening to them" (Acts 16:25). Joy in adversity is one of the most potent factors in being a living witness for Christ.

7. It was a reverent church

Although the early Church's worship was often informal and spontaneous, it was not irreverent. Luke emphasizes this fact:

> Everyone was filled with awe.
>
> (Acts 2:43)

The apostles, by the power of the Spirit, were able to perform the same kind of miracles as Jesus. Thus all the people were conscious of God's presence and many converts were added to the Church.

Supernatural power was very evident on several occasions, none more so than in the account of the sudden deaths of Ananias and Sapphira (Acts 5:1–10). Their severe punishment is for some people extremely difficult to comprehend. Why were they not given the opportunity to repent like so many others? Surely Peter could have returned their money and expelled them from the Church. Why was this sin so serious? The answer is that if their hypocrisy had been allowed to go unchecked, it would have seriously retarded the growth of Christianity in its infancy.

The realization that God's judgment had struck resulted in a great fear coming upon the whole Church and upon all who heard about what happened. As a result, the integrity of the Church was preserved and it continued to grow unabated in this important formative period. The supernatural power that had been manifest at Pentecost was still active and would continue to demonstrate the awesomeness of God. This should be a constant reminder to us that God is so great and powerful that we should come before Him with reverent obedience. The Psalmist says,

> ... the LORD delights in those who fear him,
>   who put their hope in his unfailing love.

> (Psalm 147:11)

Such fear puts all other fears into perspective and also enables us to worship the holiness of God reverently.

8. It was a growing church

A casual glance at Acts 2:42–47 could give the impression that the early Church only studied the apostles' teaching, worshipped God, and cared entirely for its own members. It appears to be totally segregated and uninterested in the plight of those outside the Christian community. This was not so, for the believers were also very much committed to welcoming others into fellowship as we see from verse 47.

> And the Lord added to their number daily those who were being saved.
>
> (Acts 2:47)

The sound teaching and the witness of the Church members, shown by their exuberant love for God and their practical love to each other, was undoubtedly a powerful testimony. But that alone could never truly save anyone. It is the Lord (that is, Jesus Christ) who turns a sinner into a saint. He alone can add new members to His Church. That is why, when a person is saved, he or she thanks the Lord Jesus Christ.

People were being added daily to the early Church, which suggests that evangelism was not an intermittent occurrence. The early Christians had a tremendous and ongoing witness, shown both by what they said and the attractiveness of their actions. As a result of this, more and more people accepted Jesus as their Lord and Savior. Churches now sometimes organize an annual "outreach week" (or month), and such events are commendable, but only so long as they are a part of a continuous program (see chapter 3).

Concluding thoughts

The outstanding characteristics of the New Testament Church are all based upon relationships. First there is a reconciliation to God, which then leads inevitably to a heartfelt relationship with others. Christians must never think of themselves as independent from the Body of Christ, but instead realize they are all one because of their common relationship with God. Undoubtedly, a Spirit-filled church will be a learning, sharing, caring, praying, worshipping, joyful, reverent, and evangelizing church. It will be a supernatural church. May our gracious God fill us with the desire and the power for that kind of church!

To think about and discuss

1. What are the marks and practical consequences of being filled with the Spirit?

2. Do you enjoy being with other Christians? What responsibilities do Christians within a local fellowship have towards one another?

3. Consider how you personally, and your church corporately, would be evaluated according to the characteristics revealed in Acts 2:42–47.

4. Read Matthew 6:9–13 and consider what vital lessons this passage teaches us about how to pray.

5. Why is worship important to the life of a Christian? How do I make worship a part of my life?

6. How would you answer someone who said that the Church's major priority should be evangelism? What are the consequences of such an attitude?

CHAPTER 2

A Shared Ministry

The early years of the Christian Church were a period of great excitement and rapid numerical growth. But clouds were gathering on the horizon and it would soon experience serious problems. Physical opposition from without and troubles that surfaced within would become a recurring threat.

Sometimes even mundane practical matters can lead to tensions between groups, and the New Testament Church was not exempt from these.

> The Grecian Jews among them complained against the Hebraic Jews because their widows were being overlooked in the daily distribution of food.
>
> (Acts 6:1)

This was a very subtle attack by the devil to destroy the Church by preoccupying the apostles with work which was not their God-given responsibility. Their primary calling was to devote themselves to prayer and to ministering the Word in preaching and teaching. A dereliction of these duties because of excessive social administration would have been disadvantageous and perhaps fatal to the growth of the infant Church.

A problem arose which needed to be dealt with quickly and wisely. There is no suggestion that the unfair distribution of food was deliberate; it was probably a result of poor administration or a lack of supervision. No one was in charge and so a case of injustice occurred which could have easily resulted in a catastrophic division within the fellowship. Sometimes today, there are groups in the Church who can easily be unintentionally overlooked. People such as the young, the old, the single, ethnic minorities, newcomers, and even those who have been in membership for many years can be neglected. Large fellowships or those experiencing rapid numerical growth are especially vulnerable to such negligence. Wherever and whenever discrimination occurs, it urgently needs to be rectified, for if it is ignored or overlooked, the Church will surely suffer.

Responding to the challenge

Running away from difficult situations by evading facts or treating them with complacency is never a positive way forward. Despite this, there are those who are reluctant to acknowledge problems because they can be extremely difficult and painful to resolve. Some adopt this policy in relation to their health. Rather than confronting an illness by immediately going to the doctor, they hope that it will go away. There is a tendency to take the line of least resistance with any problem that frightens us, but to do so is usually a serious error. "A stitch in time saves nine" is a well-known proverb that should be heeded and practiced, for it offers sound advice. The apostles were wise not to ignore the plight of the Grecian Jews and say, "Don't worry about it. Probably the situation will get better." Instead the problem was resolved quickly, efficiently, and in an attitude of love.

Sometimes there can be a great temptation for God's servants to run away from a difficult situation. This was Jonah's reaction when faced with the task of preaching to Israel's enemies, the people of Nineveh. He tried to evade his obvious responsibilities by boarding a boat for Tarshish (modern Spain), even though he knew that ultimately it was impossible to escape God. Jonah's flight from God bears testimony to the frequency with which such tragedies occur among us. It is so easy to be guided by circumstances and ignore God's infallible Word.

Another common mistake when responding to a crisis is to panic, for this will inevitably do more harm than good. Focusing excessively on the negative possibilities of what may happen and ignoring the positive potential of God's capabilities is wrong. We should never be overwhelmed by the size of any problem, because we know that our God is in control of every situation. Therefore,

> Cast your cares on the LORD
> and he will sustain you;
> he will never let the righteous fall. (Psalm 55:22)

There are several accounts throughout the Bible of men and women who kept calm when faced with a crisis. For instance, Abigail forestalling David's wrath (1 Samuel 25:1–35), and Mordecai when faced with the threatened destruction of his people (Esther 4). In the New Testament we see that Paul, after days at sea in hurricane-force winds and facing unavoidable shipwreck, says to the others on board,

> "For the last fourteen days," he said, "you have been in constant suspense and have gone without food – you haven't eaten anything. Now I urge you to take some food. You need it to survive. Not one of you will lose a single hair from his head."
>
> (Acts 27:33–34)

Paul remained calm whilst others around him were in a state of turmoil.

Confidence comes from being constantly aware of the presence, power, and provision of God. This should be a characteristic of all who have faith in Jesus, but regrettably, churches frequently fail to tackle all kinds of problems. Irregular attendance, undisciplined children, hostility between individuals, doubtful business dealings, and romantic involvement with unbelievers are just a few examples. There are many other situations where taking action may be truly painful, but the consequences of doing nothing are far worse.

Reactions to adversity are the real test of leadership. The novelist Joseph Conrad recalled an occasion when he was a young man and was learning to steer a sailing-ship. A gale blew up, and his experienced teacher gave him just one piece of advice: "Keep her facing it. Always keep her facing it." Likewise leaders must be prepared to face whatever dangers might threaten.

The appointing of the Seven

There are several principles in Acts 6:1–7 that are applicable to the Church in every generation. First, there is the vital principle of suitable management, whereby you choose a structure that matches the need. It is always important to question the way that things are done so as to discover what changes, if any, need to be made. Paradoxically, problems may even be beneficial in that they provide opportunities to examine the way that we do things.

The second principle illustrated in this incident is that of diverse ministries. The apostles quickly realized that they could not do everything by themselves and that it was essential to share with others the responsibility of running the

Church. It is a fact that God calls people to different ministries and so omnicompetence in leadership skills ought not to be expected or demanded. There is no church that God intends to have only one minister. Hence, it is a great mistake to refer to the pastorate as "the ministry", for the term implies that it is the only ministry there is.

An acquaintance once told me that his church, when seeking a leader, desired four major attributes. The candidate should be an exceptional preacher, an excellent pastor, an efficient administrator, and able to work effectively with young people. This acquaintance was of the opinion that if you found someone possessing one of these gifts, your church would stay about the same. If you found someone with two of these gifts, your church would probably grow. If it was possible to find someone with three of these gifts, you would be the most popular church in your area. And if you could find someone with all four gifts, you should avoid him because he was probably a freak.

For a church to be successful it needs a multiplicity of gifts which no one individual can provide. Yet, irrespective of this truth, churches frequently search for and expect to find someone who possesses every gift. Initially, it may appear they have found such a person, but the situation won't last – for the simple reason that God's way of doing things is by a shared ministry. The apostles realized this and rightly delegated the responsibility for the daily distribution of food to others, so that they themselves were not distracted from their priorities.

Personal expectations

A common occurrence within the Church is that its leaders become overwhelmed with their workload and, as a result, experience premature burn-out, unsatisfying "survival," or a nervous breakdown. Those who ignore their limitations fail; they always have and they always will. Despite this truth, there are many leaders who will boldly say, "I'd rather burn out than rust out in the service of the Lord." Such an attitude is a mistake because surely burn-out is not what God wants for us. A comment by James Berkeley outlines an excellent alternative:

> *I admire the bravado. It sounds dedicated, bold, and stirring. However, when I view the burn-outs and the almost burn-outs who lie by the ecclesiastical road, the glory fails to reach me. I see pain and waste and unfinished service. Is there not a third alternative to either burning out or rusting out? In Acts 20:24, Paul stated, "I consider my life worth nothing to me, if only I may finish the race and complete the task the Lord Jesus has given me." Herein lies the model I choose to follow. I want neither to burn out nor rust out. I want to finish out the race.*[1]

Occasionally, overworked leaders only have themselves to blame because they are unwilling to show faith in others to get the best out of them. Of course it can also be the fault of those under them in that they expect their leaders to do everything. Some would unashamedly say, "Isn't that what they're paid for?" In both situations the consequences are disastrous. First, the standard of preaching and teaching will decline because the leaders will have inadequate time for prayer and study. Second, the other members will not be given the opportunity to exercise or develop their own God-given gifts.

Realizing your limitations

Because of their extreme workload, the apostles called a
meeting of all the believers and said,

> "Brothers, choose seven men from among you who are
> known to be full of the Spirit and wisdom. We will turn this
> responsibility over to them."
>
> (Acts 6:3)

They were not suggesting that the practical administration
of welfare is an inferior work. It is entirely a matter of calling. These Seven would free the apostles for their primary
task of spending time in prayer and ministering the Word
of God.

It should be noticed that the apostles had faith in the
membership to recommend those who were suitable for
these practical responsibilities. They did not impose a solution upon the Church but simply made a proposal, suggesting
the required number that was needed for this particular
predicament and naming the necessary qualifications. This
is an instance of the whole body of believers being given
responsibility within the early Church, though presumably
the apostles reserved the right to veto an unwise choice, for it
was essential that the Seven chosen would have a good reputation and be "full of the Spirit and wisdom." Only then would
they have the spiritual insight to reach correct solutions.

Those selected were then commissioned for their
special ministry by the apostles with prayer and the
laying-on of hands, thus imparting the blessing or
good will of the fellowship that was necessary for this
important work. This action does not suggest anything
mystical nor in this instance did it impart the gift of the
Spirit; the Seven were filled with the Holy Spirit prior to
being chosen.

Although their chief responsibility was to deal with the practical matters of administration, it is evident that the activities of some were not confined to this. Philip, not to be confused with the apostle of that name, was a gifted evangelist, whilst Stephen, a man full of God's grace and power, exercised a preaching ministry. They were well equipped for public leadership in general and obviously had gifts that extended beyond their specific office.

The direct result of the action of the apostles in delegating the social work so as to focus on their priorities of prayer and preaching was that the Word of God spread.

> The number of disciples in Jerusalem increased rapidly, and a large number of priests became obedient to the faith.
>
> (Acts 6:7)

This implies that the settlement of the dispute and the recognition of responsibilities within the Church allowed the apostles to concentrate their efforts where they were most needed.

There are times when Christians bring to the attention of their leaders matters which are quite inconsequential. Like anyone else, Christians can become obsessed with trivia. However, when a genuine problem is identified it should be addressed promptly and with love. It is noticeable that the apostles did not take offense at the complaint from the Grecian Jews and neither does it appear that the Hebraic Jews took umbrage. The apostles realized their limitations and promptly sought help so that the problem was harmoniously resolved.

Church government

There are those who believe that the appointment of
the Seven constitutes the conception of the diaconate,
because the work for which these men were chosen
is clearly indicated. Others would argue that the Seven
are nowhere described as deacons by Luke and that he
uses the word *diakonia* in this instance both for the distribution of relief (Acts 6:1) and for the "ministry of the
word" by the apostles (Acts 6:4). Certainly, deacons were
recognized in the early Church (Philippians 1:1), but
whether the Seven belonged to this category or were a
distinct body is debatable.

My own belief is that, scripturally, the individual church
is governed by a plurality of elders (Acts 14:23; James 5:14)
who should remain permanently in office unless there are
valid reasons for termination. A full-time pastor should not be
considered to hold a unique office and therefore allowed
to rule alone; the Bible does not permit such a distinction.
Every elder, despite the different functions that he performs, is equally responsible for the spiritual ministry of
the church.

It is tragic that, occasionally, power struggles occur
in churches over who should be in charge and so some
people are of the opinion that a collective ministry cannot
work. They believe that it is impossible to have more than
one leader and maintain a strong unity. On the contrary, I
am of the opinion that there should be no irreparable division or dissension if the elders are preeminently men of
God and are thus able to apply the Scripture to their everyday life. Regrettably, there are some very gifted men who
prove to be spiritually immature and unsuitable for leading
others in the Christian life.

Scriptural qualifications for elders

Strict qualifications must be observed during the selection process of elders and these are outlined by Paul in two key New Testament passages: 1 Timothy 3:2–7 and Titus 1:6–9. It is not my intention to produce a detailed exegesis of these but rather to focus upon the salient points that must be considered when evaluating candidates for leadership.

First, an overseer must be "above reproach" (1 Timothy 3:2). This is not to say that he must be perfect. If that were so, there would be no leaders, for all have sinned and continually fall short of God's glorious standard. The principle is simply that he should strive to live a blameless life to the glory of God and show a constant concern for the welfare of others. His lifestyle must be such that it is not justifiably possible to accuse him of behavior which is inappropriate for a mature Christian.

Anyone who seeks personal popularity, power, or praise is totally unsuitable to lead. Such a man would be wise to heed the words that the prophet Jeremiah spoke to Baruch:

> Should you then seek great things for yourself?
> Seek them not.
>
> (Jeremiah 45:5)

Men ought to desire and actively seek the privilege of leadership, for it is a noble task, providing that the only motivation is to serve God and His people. Oswald Sanders in his book *Spiritual Leadership* expressed this well:

> *The real spiritual leader is focused on the service he and she can render to God and other people, not on residuals and perks*

*of high office or holy title. We must aim to put more into life
than we take out.*[2]

In Jesus we see that God's leadership is self-sacrificial, willing to sacrifice so much to care for and save His sheep from everlasting destruction. Jesus says,

I am the good shepherd. The good shepherd lays down his life for the sheep.

(John 10:11)

To put the interests of others first is a sign of Christlikeness and an essential quality of any good leader.

Paul's comments in his first letter to Timothy and to Titus enable us to compile a list of essential qualities for candidates seeking the office of eldership which should be carefully and prayerfully studied. Certainly, he must not be a recent convert, a so-called babe in the faith, but someone experienced in sound doctrine and practice. He must have experienced many of the challenges of church life so as to be prepared to withstand the great pressures of responsibility. Whatever the situation, he must be able to encourage others with sound gospel teaching and show to those who oppose it where they are wrong.

As to his family life, he must be a one-woman man. He is devoted to his wife and not distracted by other women. This is not suggesting that remarried widowers or those who are single are ineligible. Singleness may sometimes be beneficial to a ministry in that there are no family distractions. Even so, I am convinced that it would not be ideal to have an eldership composed entirely of bachelors, for the experience of marriage and family life is an important aspect of ministry.

Whether a divorced man, remarried or not, can be an elder depends upon questions such as these: Did the divorce and possible remarriage occur before he was converted? Were there valid reasons for the divorce? Was he responsible for the break-up of the original marriage? Whenever such a candidate is considered, it must be clear that his previous actions should not in any way dishonor the Name that is above every name.

When considering a married man, it is essential that he be a good family leader with a wife and, where applicable, children who respect and obey him.

> If anyone does not know how to manage his own family, how can he take care of God's church?
>
> (1 Timothy 3:5)

Hence, it usually follows that if a man has managed his family well, it is likely that he will do so for the Lord's family, the local church. Obviously, when appointing a single man, some criterion other than married life will have to be considered. Perhaps his ability to lead may be judged by how he works with others.

As to his personal qualities, he must be temperate, self-controlled, and respectable. There will be an intense desire to glorify God in all things, and the power that comes from the Holy Spirit will be at work within him.

> ... the fruit of the Spirit is ... self-control.
>
> (Galatians 5:22–23)

Personal discipline must be based on God's guidelines as found in the Bible.

Anyone who desires to be an elder must be hospitable and deeply concerned about the welfare of others. Therefore, he will welcome guests into his home. But hospitality is far more than an open door to one's home. It is to have an open heart to those in need. Without love (1 Corinthians 13:2), he fails the test of Biblical hospitality. Regular contact with every member, so as to be able to inquire into their spiritual state and minister to their individual needs, is a "must" for all elders.

He must not be susceptible to drunkenness or any kind of addiction that might take control of his life. Although the Bible does not condemn alcohol, it does emphasize the need for moderation. Deteriorating work performance, and immoral, irresponsible, and aggressive behaviors, are often signs of excessive drinking. An elder should never be violent; rather he should be gentle. Neither should he be quarrelsome. He may strongly disagree over various issues but will not be verbally abusive or contentious.

A further characteristic of a man selected for Christian leadership is that he is not addicted to the love of wealth, for greed ruins relationships. This is why Jesus says,

> "No servant can serve two masters. Either he will hate the one and love the other, or he will be devoted to the one and despise the other. You cannot serve both God and Money."
>
> (Luke 16:13)

A leader may be a successful and wealthy businessman, but he must not be a slave to anything or anyone except Christ Jesus. There must be a spontaneous and enthusiastic desire to honor God and care for His people.

It should be remembered that elders are made by God, not by men (Acts 20:28), though the individual church is responsible for recognizing the emergence of those whom the Holy Spirit has prepared and set apart. As a result of this, it is as wrong to pass by the obviously God-made man as it is to appoint scripturally unqualified men to this office. Sadly, gifted men are often overlooked for various unscriptural reasons, and a church that does this will inevitably suffer. If God has laid His hand on a man and equipped him for such a ministry, it is the church's duty to recognize this. To do otherwise is blatantly to disobey the will of God.

The fact that God makes men elders means that it is not possible to determine in advance how many elders a church will have. Quality is more important than quantity and so there must be no lowering of standards in order to attain a necessary quota. Hastily installing men – for whatever reason – who were never called and equipped by God is extreme folly and so must be avoided. I once saw a car sticker that said, "Don't follow me – I'm lost too." That is the state of all Christian leaders who are not chosen by God.

When considering the qualifications for eldership it must be appreciated that no one will be perfect in every particular, for not even elders are completely sanctified. Those we are looking for are godly, mature men who strive to live blameless lives and are morally pure so that they set an example for others to follow.

The quality of leadership will greatly influence the strength and spiritual growth of the Body of Christ. Consequently, one of the first things that Paul did was to appoint elders in every church as under-shepherds of God's people (Acts 14:23). That is why the Church today urgently needs such saints and servants who are first and foremost men of God.

Shortage or surplus

The ideal situation is to be ruled by a plurality of elders, but in reality this might not be an immediate possibility. There are churches that have only one elder – and some may have none. What then are we to do in such situations? Since God is the one who qualifies men to the ministry of elders (and also deacons), it is necessary to recognize only those who have been prepared by the Holy

Spirit. Urgent prayer that suitable men will emerge from within the membership or be provided from elsewhere is crucial.

Where the Lord has provided a church with more elders and deacons than the work requires, it may be an indication that these surplus gifts should be used elsewhere. This may result in the formation of another church or the provision of help to weaker churches. Whatever the response, it is essential that all gifts are fully utilized for God's glory and service.

The role of deacons

Besides elders, the other office to be ordained by God is that of deacons, whose qualifications are listed in 1 Timothy 3:8–13. It will be noticed that the requirements are almost identical to those demanded of elders.

Therefore, Paul says,

> Deacons, likewise, are to be men worthy of respect.
>
> (1 Timothy 3:8)

The primary difference is that elders must be able to teach, and they have a special responsibility for shepherding the people of God, whilst deacons are primarily responsible for the practical administration and social welfare of the church.

The early Church selected deacons who were skilled in working with people. Today they are often chosen for their skill in business management and finance. However, these attributes alone are insufficient for the true ministry of a deacon. Before men are appointed as deacons, they should be given other duties in the church as a test of their ability and character. Then if they do well and prove themselves to be scripturally qualified, they may serve as deacons.

The work of women (or deaconesses)

It has often been said that Paul was a misogynist because he wrote such things as:

> ... women should remain silent in the churches. They are not allowed to speak, but must be in submission, as the Law says.

(1 Corinthians 14:34)

Others would argue that he endorses the importance of servant-women (or deaconesses) within the Church (1 Timothy 3:11). This is a verse upon which commentators disagree. Are these women workers the "wives" of deacons (as in NIV) or "deaconesses" (NIV margin)? Either translation can be correct, though Paul probably uses the word in the latter sense. If he was referring to those women who were married to deacons, then it appears strange that he did not also outline the role for the wives of elders.

God made men and women different and, though both are equal before God (Galatians 3:28), they have been given different roles.

> ... man did not come from woman, but woman from man; neither was man created for woman, but woman for man.

(1 Corinthians 11:8–9)

Although the Scriptures clearly teach the headship of man, the gifts of women are to be recognized and used. There are many examples within Acts of the significant role played by women in the spread of the gospel: Dorcas, Lydia, Priscilla, the four daughters of Philip who had the gift of prophecy, and many others. Phoebe (Romans 16:1), who faithfully served the church in Cenchrea, is consequently called a "servant" (*diakonos*) of that fellowship. The word *diakonos* can also be used in a more specialized sense. In 1 Timothy 3:8 it refers, in the plural, to deacons. Does this perhaps mean that Paul attributes to Phoebe the ecclesiastical office of deaconess? Opinion on this is divided.

Doubtless there were women who performed very important special ministries within the early Church, despite the fact that it was very much a man's world. Then, as now, there are certain roles which would be difficult or unwise for a man to fulfill by himself. Hence, women who are worthy of respect, who are temperate and trustworthy in everything they do, are always essential for the building of God's Kingdom.

One body with many parts

Even though we may never occupy a position of leadership within the Church, we are all called upon to be active servants of Jesus Christ. The Holy Spirit neglects no Christian, for each is allocated a gift or gifts which are to be used for the glory of God. Everyone without exception has a role to fulfill. That is why Paul likens the Church to a human body (1 Corinthians 12:12–31), which is a complex and diversified organism. Each part performs its own distinct function but nevertheless is essential to the effective working of the entire body. Similarly, the Church consists of many different members who are necessary for the benefit of each other and thus the Church.

It appears that in many fellowships a faithful few do most of the work, whilst others, except for attending when convenient, are idle. Such members should realize that God will ultimately hold them accountable for everything they do or fail to do. Some make the mistake of joining a church without first carefully considering the privileges and the responsibilities. The diverse gifts which God has graciously given are to be used within the Christian community and for the common good of humanity at every opportunity.

Those in pastoral oversight have a duty to recognize and help develop the gifts of every individual (see Ephesians 4:12). They are not to guard their position jealously and thus monopolize the church. Rather, the aim must be to recognize the distinctive function of every member so that all are usefully engaged in spiritual labor. Otherwise, some people will stagnate, or become restless and start searching for greener pastures.

Christians are not to be passengers but members of the crew. All will be actively involved in a spiritual battle with the united aim of rendering service to each other and to the Church. Like Paul at the end of his life, may we be able to say,

> I have fought the good fight, I have finished the race, I have kept the faith.
>
> (2 Timothy 4:7)

To those who do, God has promised to give the crown of righteousness – a victor's crown!

To think about and discuss

1. Discuss the practical problems that might arise following a vast influx of new members. How could such problems be resolved?

2. What was the attitude of the early Church towards the social needs of its members? Is this a model for Spirit-filled communities to follow?

3. All Christians are meant to be workers. Yet, being human, we need to realize our physical limitations. Why is self-care important? What would it not be right for me to continue doing, or start doing?

4. Paul says that an overseer "must be above reproach" (1 Timothy 3:2). What does he mean? And what doesn't he mean?

5. Why is good leadership vital? How should we treat our leaders? (See Hebrews 13:17.)

6. All Christians possess a gift or gifts which are to be used serving God and His people. To what extent is this true of your church?

Notes

1 Paul D. Robbins (ed.), *When It's Time to Move: A Guide to Changing Churches*, Leadership Library, vol. 4 (Word Books, 1985), p. 154.

2 J. Oswald Sanders, *Spiritual Leadership: Principles of Excellence for Every Believer* (Moody Publishers, 2007), p. 14.

—≈—

CHAPTER 3

New Testament Patterns for Evangelism and Church Planting

The book of Acts clearly reveals how New Testament churches came into being and rapidly spread. Hence, much can be gained by examining what the early Christians did and why they had such a tremendous impact upon society. Admittedly, their situation was in many ways considerably different from our own, but there are also similarities applicable to evangelism and church planting which should be emulated in every place and generation.

Initially, all the attention is focused on Jerusalem where about 3,000 people believed what Peter said and were baptized and added to the Church (Acts 2:41). As a result, the number of Christians in Jerusalem grew from 120 to over 3,000 in one day. Every level of society had been confronted with the straightforward proclamation of the resurrection of Christ, so Christianity could not be ignored. Furthermore, this phenomenal growth due to the outpouring of the Holy Spirit continued unabated (Acts 4:4; 5:14; 6:1, 7), so that a reasonable estimate would suggest that there were more than 20,000 Christians in Jerusalem just prior to the martyrdom of Stephen. Then, and now, people are changed as the Spirit enters their lives.

Persecution scatters the believers

The spread of Christianity from Jerusalem was so successful because of a great persecution against the Church immediately following Stephen's death. Saul of Tarsus was the prime persecutor; with the authority of the Sanhedrin, he zealously attempted to destroy the followers of Jesus Christ. This resulted in "all except the apostles" being scattered throughout Judea and Samaria (Acts 8:1). In a sense, it could be said that Saul, by attempting to destroy the Church, was promoting it, because the Christians by the power of God preached the good news about Jesus with great enthusiasm wherever they went. Thus, church planting in those early days was not primarily a planned decision by Christians. Rather, it happened because of a great wave of persecution that forced them to flee from Jerusalem to neighboring regions. As the believers gathered together in new locations, churches were born.

Obviously at this stage, the early Christians did not have church buildings, so very often their evangelism and worship was of necessity done in secular territory. Often they witnessed in the open air, a practice which today is discredited by many. Some will say, "It's all right if you like that kind of thing!" This attitude prevails despite the fact that there are churches struggling to make any significant inroads into their community. They may hold evangelistic Sunday services, but only a few or no visitors attend. What's the point of an evangelistic service inside a church building if the seats are empty? Doubtless, it should be said, "If we can't get people to come in and hear the gospel, why don't we go out to them?" That is what the Bible teaches and ultimately it's our obedience that counts.

A Jewish Christian named Philip, who was also called "the evangelist" (Acts 21:8), boldly went to a city in Samaria and told the people there about Christ (Acts 8:5). This was a significant advance, for Jews did not usually associate with Samaritans due to a quarrel that went back many centuries. Even so, Philip preached the gospel to these people who were either disliked or despised by most Jews. Besides this, he performed miracles and preached with such power that many men and women were baptized in the name of the Lord. Through his ministry, people were physically and spiritually healed. No wonder there was "great joy" in this Samaritan city (Acts 8:7).

News of Philip's evangelistic work reached the apostles back in Jerusalem, and they heard that many people in Samaria had accepted God's message and expressed their faith by receiving Christian baptism. For this reason, the Church dispatched the apostles Peter and John to investigate what was happening and to provide support. At one time, John and his brother James had suggested that fire should be called down from heaven to consume a Samaritan community for their inhospitable attitude towards Jesus (Luke 9:52–55). Now (Acts 8:15) John's desire was that fire should come from heaven not to destroy them, but to fill them with the power of the Holy Spirit. When that happens, people cannot fail to notice it.

After proclaiming the Word of the Lord and doing all they could to strengthen the faith of the Samaritan believers, Peter and John returned to Jerusalem to give a report of their work and, not wanting to waste opportunities on their return journey, preached the gospel in many Samaritan villages. Earlier, this would have been inconceivable, but now it was realized that our Christian brothers and sisters are chosen by God.

Philip and the Ethiopian

A preacher must always be prepared to preach the gospel wherever God might send him, even though sometimes God's call may appear to be illogical. It would not have been unreasonable for Philip, when given a new evangelistic commission, to have questioned what might be gained by going to the desert road that runs from Jerusalem to Gaza (Acts 8:26). Surely he was doing a tremendous work in Samaria, successfully preaching to multitudes, and to leave doesn't appear to be the obvious move by any stretch of the imagination. However, Philip received a divine command to leave the crowds so that he might meet one man: an Ethiopian eunuch who had been on a pilgrimage to Jerusalem and was now returning home.

Seated in his chariot, this man was reading aloud from the book of the prophet Isaiah, and Philip heard him.

> "Do you understand what you are reading?" Philip asked.
> "How can I," he said, "unless someone explains it to me?"
> So he invited Philip to come up and sit with him.
>
> (Acts 8:30–31)

The passage of Scripture he had been reading was this:

> He was led like a sheep to the slaughter,
>   and as a lamb before the shearer is silent,
>   so he did not open his mouth.
> In his humiliation he was deprived of justice.
>   Who can speak of his descendants?
>   For his life was taken from the earth.
>
> (Acts 8:32; Isaiah 53:7–8)

Through reading this text, Philip showed him who Jesus was, and the Ethiopian believed and was baptized. Philip had gone out of his way to speak to this man and it resulted in the gospel message being taken to Africa. As for Philip, he next appears at Azotus (the Old Testament Philistine city of Ashdod) from where he made his way up the coast, preaching all the way to Caesarea, where he appears to have settled (Acts 21:8–9).

Personal conversations were a common feature of the early Church and clearly a most effective and natural means of spreading the faith. Jesus repeatedly used this method of one-to-one conversation in His ministry, thus concentrating upon specific problems and individual needs. Such personal relationships are forever a central element in introducing people to the Christian faith.

To Caesarea and Antioch

Acts 10 provides an account of the Gentile "Pentecost" when a centurion in the Roman army named Cornelius, along with his relatives and close friends, experienced the gift of the Holy Spirit. This happened whilst Peter was preaching the Word of God to them in the house of Cornelius at Caesarea. To enter a Gentile dwelling was, for a strict Jew, a distinct breach of custom. Peter, however, now a Christian, made it clear that he would not have violated his Jewish practices if God had not shown him in a vision that he should not think of anyone as impure or unclean. News of this revolutionary action – entering the home of Gentiles and eating with them – reached the apostles and other believers in Judea (Acts 11:1).

Later, Peter explained to them what had happened and those Jewish believers who had criticized him were silenced. At this stage the critics had no further objections, but only for a short while. The problem relating to circumcision would once more become a major issue for those who adhered strongly to Jewish tradition (Acts 15:1).

Again, as he had done in Acts 8:1–4, Luke refers to Stephen's death and tells how the scattering of believers that had begun at that time, due to persecution, was now spreading wider still. Phoenicia (whose major cities were Tyre and Sidon), Cyprus, and Antioch all received those who spoke the good news about Jesus (Acts 11:19). Many targeted only their fellow Jews, but there were some anonymous believers from Cyprus and Cyrene who went to the cosmopolitan city of Antioch-on-the-Orontes (i.e. the Orontes River, along which it was located) and preached to Gentiles. Because the power of the Lord was upon them, a large number of these Gentiles believed and turned to the Lord.

When the Jerusalem believers heard of this, they sent Barnabas, himself a Cypriot Jew like some of the evangelists at Antioch, to investigate and help nurture this new multicultural church. Barnabas soon realized the urgent need for more leadership within this rapidly growing situation and so he personally fetched Saul from Tarsus to help. Both of them stayed with the church in Antioch for a full year, teaching great numbers of people and strengthening the fellowship.

It was at Antioch that the followers of Jesus were first called "Christians" (Acts 11:26). Prior to that, Luke has referred to them in Acts as "brothers" (1:16; 9:30), those "being saved" (2:47), "disciples" (6:1), the people of "the Way" (9:2), "saints" (9:13) and "believers" (10:45). The title "Christian" began as a nickname given by the unbelieving Gentiles of Antioch who were famed for their readiness in giving names. When the bearded emperor Julian came to visit them, they nicknamed him "the Goat." To be called "Christians" says something about how the believers were regarded in Antioch. At the very least, it shows that people were impressed by the fact that Jesus Christ was the main subject of their conversations.

It is no exaggeration to say that the conversion of Gentiles at Antioch is one of the greatest events in history. For the first time, the gospel is intentionally taken to Gentiles. All the previous instances have been leading to this momentous step forward. Previously, Philip had preached to the Samaritans; but they were half-Jewish. Then Peter had witnessed to Cornelius; though this was at the request of Cornelius. Also it is clear (Acts 10:2) that Cornelius was a God-fearer and, therefore, to a limited extent an adherent of Judaism. Now, in Antioch, the Christians took the initiative and deliberately preached the gospel to people who had no connection with Judaism. Following this, Christianity would develop worldwide.

Paul's first missionary journey

Antioch, which was the capital of the province of Syria, and the third greatest city in the world after Rome and Alexandria, became an important center of Christianity. It is from here that Paul, under the direct guidance of the Holy Spirit, sets out with Barnabas on the first of his important missionary, church-planting journeys. Earlier he had witnessed in Syria and Cilicia (Galatians 1:21), but we can call the departure mentioned in Acts 13:1–3 the beginning of his first official missionary journey, since he is now an accredited agent of the church at Antioch, sent to work among Gentiles.

The concept of a missionary – or indeed any Christian – who is not in membership with a church is contrary to New Testament practice. John Wesley rightly said, "There is nothing less Christian than a solitary Christian." The sending body of a missionary should always be the local church – a point that is made abundantly clear (see Acts 13:1–3; 14:26–28; 15:40). That is not to say that the responsibilities cannot be shared with other churches, friends, or a missionary society, but the prime responsibility remains with the church of which the missionary is a member. The individualistic freelancers who are common in the twenty-first century are working contrary to New Testament practice. Paul and Barnabas did not act unilaterally in any way, apart from the Church, but were set apart and sent out to do a special work.

On their return, Paul and Barnabas gave a report to their church at Antioch (Acts 14:27) of all the great things God had done, and also informed other churches (Acts 15:3–4). Obviously there was a strong sense of corporate fellowship between the churches. Returning to Antioch again, they, along with many others, taught and preached the Word of the Lord.

Some time later, Paul wanted to go back to each place where he had previously preached to see how the new believers were progressing. Barnabas would have gone with him except for a sharp disagreement over who should go with them (Acts 15:39). Hence, they acrimoniously parted company and went their separate ways. Silas became Paul's companion for this second missionary tour, whilst Barnabas went to Cyprus with John Mark (see chapter 4).

After returning and spending an unspecified time in Antioch, Paul left on his third and last mission. It centers upon the events at Ephesus, but also included evangelistic activity in Galatia and Phrygia, as well as in Macedonia and Achaia. This was not new territory for Paul and so he was providing help and encouragement to the churches rather than being involved in pioneer evangelism.

The New Testament pattern clearly reveals that outreach is a priority of every church. The stark choice is to evangelize or fossilize. There is no alternative. Paul's strategy was to evangelize and plant churches to which, in due course, he appointed elders, as in Acts 14:23. When he had accomplished this, he moved on. This should be our strategy too, for it is the most effective way of reaching unbelievers.

It is noticeable that Paul rarely traveled alone and that his missionary journeys involved teamwork. This is a stark contrast to the one-man ministry so often encountered today. Teams have several advantages: the counterbalancing of extremes; a greater range of gifts; more workers to share the load; fellowship whereby members bear one another's burdens; and the opportunity to train young and inexperienced men and women. Even Jesus gathered a group around Him, thus setting an example for us to follow.

The local church and church planting

Numerous excuses can be found to suggest that the time is not yet right for a church-planting initiative. Paul could easily have thought that his strong disagreement with Barnabas, his responsibilities within the church at Antioch, or the rapid expansion of the existing churches (Acts 16:5), meant that he should remain where he was. Despite all this, he ventured out again on a church-planting mission.

There are those who would argue that our situation is different. Don't we already have sufficient churches that can easily accommodate lots of new people? Why not fill them before building any new ones? Wouldn't it be better to first help those churches that are struggling? Surely a new church will take people from established congregations and so reduce their effectiveness. We need larger churches, not more churches. Why don't we just leave things as they are? Such suggestions appear to be logical to many people, but they are not valid reasons for permanently avoiding new ventures.

The Great Commission (Matthew 28:19–20) is not just to "go and make disciples of all nations" but to baptize them. Also, baptism must be followed by an ongoing and earnest study of the Scriptures. Peter follows Jesus' directives (Acts 2:41–42). He immediately baptizes those who believe and then, with the other apostles, teaches them the gospel of Christ. This differs from much modern evangelism which aims to get a "decision" for Christ and nothing more. No provision is made for continuing church fellowship and teaching, factors that are essential for spiritual development. Undoubtedly, the great evangelistic challenge of the New Testament is to plant churches.

When should a church consider planting a new one?

Within evangelical circles it is often suggested that when a church reaches a certain size, it should accept the opportunity to plant a new fellowship elsewhere. Otherwise, intimate and meaningful fellowship may become impractical and furthermore there might be a surfeit of people with gifts which are not effectively used. A large church can very easily become complacent and usually has a much greater percentage of "passengers" in its membership than a relatively small church. Consequently, it could be strongly argued that a rapidly growing church should constantly be seeking opportunities to spread so as to prevent it becoming numerically inefficient.

There is no universally agreed set of rules for church planting and any planning must always allow for flexibility. Many leaders who are actively involved in church planting believe that in order for the church's fellowship and pastoral care to be a practical possibility, between 100 and 150 members is likely the maximum size for membership. Personally, I am of the opinion that such reasoning probably oversimplifies the situation, for it takes no account of the make-up of the membership. For instance, a church may contain a large proportion of students, who are likely to be transitory. Or there may be many new converts who need time to develop in their Christian lives. Numerous factors must be considered before taking the important step of planting a new work, for undoubtedly, poor planning and preparation are responsible for many failures.

Although strategic planning is an essential factor, there is no substitute for wisdom in understanding God's way and will. For that reason, frequent fervent prayer is an integral part of the whole process. The believers in Antioch fasted and prayed, and the Holy Spirit made known His will to them:

> "Set apart for me Barnabas and Saul for the work to which I have called them."
>
> (Acts 13:2)

A major consideration must always be the quality of the leadership that is available. It cannot be emphasized too strongly that when it comes to church planting, leadership is the crucial issue. The church at Antioch released Barnabas and Saul, who were very gifted leaders that meant so much to them. This must have been a great sacrifice for the fellowship, even though there were other able men such as Simeon, Lucius, and Manaen to continue the original work. All planting churches must carefully consider the cost of releasing some of their best workers and recognize the unavoidable loss of close friendships. Church planting in the New Testament is chiefly, though not entirely, about planting leaders.

Established churches are sometimes reluctant to encourage those with leadership capabilities or may even actively resist them because they are considered to be unsuitable within a traditional setting. Therefore, innovative, creative, and adventurous leaders may never have the opportunity to utilize their God-given gifts unless they move elsewhere. Newly formed congregations often tend to be more receptive to courageous evangelistic challenges and, by providing opportunities, attract many leaders who display great confidence and commitment based solely on the assurance of God's presence.

A major theme of Acts is the divisions that existed within the early Church, and Paul's letters repeatedly address this problem. Although this will be dealt with more fully in the next chapter, it is mentioned here because splits within churches occur frequently today and are a source of numerous new church-planting endeavors. The underlying factors responsible for a split may develop over a number of years, or the division may arise suddenly, especially when a church degenerates into separate groups of ambitious people who are seeking personal power and prestige. Sometimes, when there are differences of opinion, the mutual separation of members into a new church can be desirable, and both the original and the new work will thrive. On the other hand, unfriendly and even bitter splits only promote resentment; frequently the dysfunctional character traits are carried forward, unlike in a Spirit-filled community whose members will spontaneously exhibit unanimity in the desire to serve the risen Christ and each other.

Where should we plant more churches?

A casual glance reveals that the primary message of Acts is the work of the Holy Spirit, without which conversions within the early Church would have been impossible. The Christians were very aware that the Spirit of Jesus dwelt amongst them and that He energized their outreach. It is the Spirit alone who enables His people to be in the right place at the right time and who, through the Word of God, turns sinners into saints. The initiative of mission always lies with God.

Before ever attempting to plant a church, it is necessary to seek God's guidance through prayer. Laborers must ask where God wants them to work and what they should do. Discovering God's will is always the major priority in allowing Him to accomplish His plans for you. From the beginning, a new church must develop as a people of prayer.

How did Paul, Silas, and their companions know where to preach the gospel? Acts 16:6–10 clearly reveals that on this occasion the Holy Spirit prevented them from speaking in some places. How this prohibition was communicated is not known; maybe it was through prophetic utterance; it may have been by a vision; it may have been the result of external circumstances or of some inner conviction. Whatever the reason, the guidance of the Spirit was paramount in determining Paul's evangelistic activity. Only when they reached Troas did they receive a positive lead.

During the night Paul had a vision of a man of Macedonia standing and begging him, "Come over to Macedonia and help us." After Paul had seen the vision, we got ready at once to leave for Macedonia, concluding that God had called us to preach the gospel to them.

(Acts 16:9–10)

Paul's success can be attributed to his exceptional enthusiasm, strategic planning, and primarily his awareness of the Holy Spirit's leading. Christians today need that guidance, as they are often confronted with far too many opportunities and innumerable possibilities. Inevitably, some doors will close whilst others open. So many mistakenly believe that they themselves may decide where to work, but that decision is God's and not ours.

A situation often arises where a church has a significant number of members living in a particular geographical location. This means that there will be an existing group of people who are familiar with their local community and doubtless already have several well-established contacts. Therefore, it is a useful exercise for a church to regularly analyze the distribution of its membership to see if there is the basis for a new outreach. This is often called "progression church planting."

Initially, such a work may take the form of a weekly Bible study, a prayer meeting, and evangelization within the neighborhood, prior to considering Sunday worship services. The great advantage of this is that it allows the available resources to be used most effectively in seeking new converts. Consequently, some experienced church planters would advocate that a Sunday-centered worship service should start only when there is a viable fellowship of believers who can function independently of other churches. Obviously, each situation will be different and it may be possible in some instances for a work to become an autonomous and independent church from the outset, though it must be emphasized that this would be the exception rather than the rule. Premature independence from the mother church is a common cause of failure.

That the gospel should be preached to all nations is a command of the risen Christ. Therefore, a growing church must seriously consider sending missionaries to areas, either at home or abroad, where the Christian faith is not already represented. Such a work may be done in conjunction with other like-minded churches so as to share the burden. Going where no one has gone before means that the team will be involved in a "parachute" or "pioneer" plant – appropriate terms, because reaching into areas where there is little or no existing support is as difficult as "pioneering" new territory. Contacts will have to be made through starting projects such as a drop-in center or meetings that are relevant and accessible to seekers. What types of publicity are most effective in your area? What does your community enjoy that might be used in your outreach? Such questions should always be asked so as to learn as much as you can. Perhaps becoming actively involved in established communal activities is a useful way to build awareness and start conversations. Such a great challenge often results in a great reward, but this form of evangelism is certainly not for the faint-hearted.

The "sending churches" should not unduly interfere with the activity of their missionaries but have confidence in those they send out. Although a degree of independence is important, the danger of isolationism must be avoided. The "go-it-alone" spirit of some churches is not what the Bible teaches. Frequent reports should be expected and regular visits between churches are to be recommended.

When pioneering new territory, it is wise to ascertain that God is not already at work. Competing with another gospel-based church, just because it is of a different denomination, implies that it is our style of worship rather than Christ that is the answer. Such an attitude can undermine the unity of the Church and suggest to unbelievers that Christians cannot agree amongst themselves. Are we building our own empire rather than the Kingdom of God?

Where there are very small, struggling gospel-based churches already in existence, it may be considered appropriate to help build what is already there. The provision of finance and/or people can be an effective means of bringing renewal and revival to the community being served. Stronger churches should be prepared to offer help, and the small church should recognize its precarious state and seek help before it is too late, even though in some instances this may mean that it ceases to exist as an independent work. A sad fact is that, frequently, struggling churches do nothing about their precarious condition and eventually close.

Considering the difficulties, it might be argued that it is easier to start from scratch than to work with a church that perhaps has difficult members and deeply entrenched traditions which cannot be substantiated from Scripture. You need to be very clear about what you might be taking on. Isn't it far easier to bring to birth than to resurrect the dead? Nevertheless, helping existing small churches can prove to be a mutually advantageous association and bring new life to the community being served.

Why do some church plants fail?

There are many factors that can cause a new work to struggle or fail, but the most common are inadequate planning and preparation. "If only I'd thought of that before we started!" This and other similar statements are common. Always be thoroughly prepared and seek advice from an experienced church planter where necessary.

Many problems result from a lack of clear leadership; in this case, struggles, quarrels, and foolishness will inevitably emerge. This was a serious problem for the church plant in Corinth, where factionalism prevailed. The people there urgently needed to focus their attention upon the solid foundation of Jesus Christ (1 Corinthians 3:1–11). Leaders must be strong and able to share their vision with those they lead and serve.

Believers today can learn the key to successful missionary activity amongst diverse cultures by studying the techniques of the apostle Paul. He adapted his teaching according to the situation. When he was with the Jews, he became one of them. When he was with the Gentiles who did not have the Jewish Law, he adapted to their circumstances. He tried to find common ground with everyone so that he might bring them to Christ (see 1 Corinthians 9:19–23). With religious Jews he used the Law to speak to them; with Gentiles he appealed to their conscience and culture. For instance, in Acts 17 he showed the philosophers in Athens that they were wrong by quoting their own poets, and then explained to them what was right. He accommodated himself to the culture and circumstances of the people to whom he preached the gospel.

This must not be taken as a license to warrant anything and everything in the name of evangelism, for Paul's "liberty" was not a freedom to sin in any way. The presentation changed but the gospel did not. It is significant that Paul had rebuked Peter for his compromise of the gospel to the Jewish brethren (Galatians 2:12–13). Paul here follows the example of Jesus, who during His earthly ministry was a friend of the worst sort of sinners, yet always observed propriety. The apostle accommodated himself to the circumstances of the people to whom he preached without compromising the gospel message. Likewise, Christians must adjust to the community in which they are placed and faithfully proclaim the gospel with a passion to win large groups of people for Christ.

A planting team must realize that extensive sowing is necessary prior to reaping and that there may be few, if any, converts in the early years. Great results often begin with great expectations but we also have to be realistic. Paul preached daily at the lecture hall of Tyrannus for two years so that people throughout the province of Asia heard the Lord's message (Acts 19:10). In Ephesus he worked hard, night and day, for three years (Acts 20:31). This resulted, however, in the formation of a church which was led by its own elders (Acts 14:23; 20:17).

Where God is active, the devil is also. As a result, it is impossible to powerfully and passionately preach the truth of the gospel of Christ and expect to avoid suffering. Opposition is inevitable, for everyone who wants to live a godly life in Christ Jesus will suffer persecution. Sometimes the devil's hostility will be subtle, but often it will be violent. Even so, evangelism and church planting are not optional extras if we pay heed to the fundamental significance of Christ's Great Commission to propagate the gospel throughout the world. The Church is, as Archbishop William Temple rightly put it, "the only society in the world that exists for the benefit of those who are not its members." There should be no greater purpose for Christians than sharing the gospel which can make an eternal difference to someone's life. The church which has no vision for outreach is not a New Testament church.

To think about and discuss

1. Why was the conversion of Gentiles at Antioch (Acts 11:19–24) such a significant advance?

2. What can missionaries today learn from Paul's strategy for evangelism and church planting?

3. Paul said,

   I have become all things to all men so that by all possible means I might save some.

   (1 Corinthians 9:22)

   What can we learn from what he did?

4. If we can't get people to come into our church buildings to hear the gospel message, why don't we go out to them? Consider the various forms of outreach that could be used.

5. Teams consist of people with different gifts, opinions, personalities, and so on. What are the advantages and disadvantages of teamwork?

6. The Great Commission tells us to make disciples of all nations by going, baptizing, and teaching people to obey all that Jesus commanded (Matthew 28:19–20). How does your church appear in the light of these verses? Why do you think this is?

CHAPTER 4

Disagreements, Divisions,
and Discipline

Christians readily acknowledge their belief in one God and
it follows from this that God's people should be united.
Paul, in his letter to the Ephesians, deals with the serious
subject of Christian unity. He writes,

> There is one body and one Spirit – just as you were called to
> one hope when you were called – one Lord, one faith, one bap-
> tism; one God and Father of all, who is over all and through all
> and in all.
>
> (Ephesians 4:4–6)

Even a casual reader cannot help but observe the repet-
ition of the word "one" which occurs seven times in these
verses. Clearly, there is one God who has only one Church.
Paul had no concept of denominations, for we are all one
in Christ Jesus. However, the truth is that even amongst
evangelical Christians, disunity is a common occurrence
within the Church. This happens despite the fact that
there should be an eagerness for some degree of visible
Christian unity between individuals and denominations,

providing that fundamental Christian truth is not sacrificed in order to achieve it.

The unity of God's people began with their common ancestry in Adam (Genesis 2), spiritual lineage through Abraham (Genesis 12), and their mass deliverance from Pharaoh's oppression through Moses (Exodus 1 – 15). According to Psalm 133, wherever there is unity in the truth, there the Lord gives His blessing. David united the twelve tribes of Israel under his kingship but later this unity fragmented. At the time of Jesus, there were various parties within Judaism. These included the Pharisees who were distinguished by their strict observance of the traditional and written Law; the Sadducees who denied the resurrection of the dead and the existence of spirits; the Zealots motivated by nationalism; and the separatist Essenes.

Differences of opinion were not confined to Judaism, for anyone who studies the pages of Acts will discover a very sad fact. The Church which had started so well soon began to experience disunity because of disagreements. Furthermore it was pressures from within and not persecution from without that was primarily responsible for this major problem. Thankfully, these differences were frequently resolved, though occasionally ideas arose which were unacceptable to the leaders of the Church and resulted in the formation of opposing groups. Divisions and struggles within and between churches are recurring features of history and so there will always be those that are divided instead of united. Who is to blame?

Humanity is responsible, not God!

Unity should be a distinguishing characteristic of the Christian community, but in practice it has always been extremely difficult to maintain. This is well illustrated by the dissension and disunity displayed within the multiethnic Corinthian church. Paul, in an attempt to bring them together, writes,

> I appeal to you, brothers, in the name of our Lord Jesus Christ, that all of you agree with one another so that there may be no divisions among you and that you may be perfectly united in mind and thought.
>
> (1 Corinthians 1:10)

In no other New Testament writing do we experience such close contact with the everyday life and problems of Christians in the first century as in this letter to the Corinthians.

The first problem that Paul deals with is the factions within the fellowship of the church which could so easily result in schism. As yet, the divisions remain within the church and Paul identifies four distinct groups of members, each claiming spiritual superiority over the others. There were those who said, "I am a follower of Paul." Others said, "I follow Apollos," or "I follow Cephas," or perhaps sanctimoniously, "I follow [only] Christ." There are those who believe that the last may not have been a group at all. They consider it to be Paul separating himself from the various factions by saying, "I belong to Christ." Even so, it is most likely that a group who claimed to be the only true Christians in Corinth had created a fourth faction within the fellowship of the church.

It should be realized that Paul, Apollos, and Cephas had in no way encouraged this attitude of divisiveness. Quite the contrary, their names had been taken without their consent, and to underline the seriousness of the situation Paul reminds the Corinthians that only Jesus' work on the cross can reconcile people to God and to each other. There is no alternative way to achieve unity than on this foundation.

Those who claimed to follow Cephas (the Jewish form of Peter's name) were probably zealous Jews who demanded that Christians must still meticulously observe Mosaic traditions, especially circumcision and the dietary regulations. That is why, when Peter returned to Jerusalem from Caesarea, the "circumcision party" criticized him and said,

> You went into the house of uncircumcised men and ate with them.
>
> (Acts 11:3)

Only when Peter explained exactly what had happened were his critics silenced. Their objections were answered and they began praising God.

Some Jewish Christians probably feared that a great influx of converts from paganism would lower the moral standards of the Church, misgivings which, according to Paul's letters, were not unfounded. Should not these Gentiles be accepted on terms like those required of proselytes to Judaism? Hence, some men came from Judea to Antioch and taught the Christians that the ancient Jewish custom of circumcision was obligatory for salvation (Acts 15:1). They had no problem with the concept of welcoming believing Gentiles into the Church providing that they were circumcised and obeyed the Law of Moses. Consequently, to become a Christian a Gentile must first become a Jew. This was a momentous problem and it would be no exaggeration to say that it could easily have resulted in Christianity becoming nothing more than a sect of Judaism.

The apostle Paul, seeing the great danger of this, argued forcefully with these legalistic Jewish teachers who were undermining the foundation of the Christian faith. They were saying that faith in Jesus alone was insufficient for salvation and, as a result of this, people were being led astray. This vital issue had to be settled.

The apostle Peter knew that God does not show favoritism but accepts all who fear Him and do what is right. Only a short while previously, God had dramatically revealed to him in a vision (Acts 10 – 11) that the customary Jewish distinction between what was "clean" and "unclean" was no longer relevant in admitting Gentiles to the Church. Regardless of this truth, he was intimidated into agreeing with those who belonged to the circumcision group that it was wrong to share fellowship with uncircumcised Gentiles. In a moment of weakness he again became a slave to legalistic obligations and thus, by imposing unnecessary rules and regulations, contradicted the truth of the gospel. That is, only faith in Jesus Christ saves a person from sin and eternal punishment in hell.

Being a recognized leader, Peter's behavior influenced others, and eventually even Barnabas was affected. The repercussions of this were that many Jewish believers in the church at Antioch would no longer eat with uncircumcised Gentile Christians and so there would inevitably be two "Lord's tables." To refuse to take Communion with other believers is to say, "I don't accept you as a Christian."

Is it possible that Peter had so soon forgotten the vision at Joppa and the conversion of Cornelius and his household? Certainly not! The fellowship in the church at Antioch was broken primarily because Peter was behaving like a hypocrite. He was momentarily afraid of offending a small but powerful pressure group and, not for the first time in his life, went back on his word. Previously he had declared to Jesus,

> I will never disown you.
>
> (Matthew 26:35)

But this was shortly followed by his complete disavowal:

I swear by God, I don't know the man!

(see Matthew 26:72; my paraphrase)

Now he was condoning segregation between Jewish and Gentile Christians, contrary to his own inner convictions.

It was because of this inconsistency of not practicing what he believed, and the terrible implications, that Paul did not hesitate to sharply rebuke him.

> When Peter came to Antioch, I opposed him to his face, because he was clearly in the wrong. Before certain men came from James, he used to eat with the Gentiles. But when they arrived, he began to draw back and separate himself from the Gentiles because he was afraid of those who belonged to the circumcision group. The other Jews joined him in his hypocrisy, so that by their hypocrisy even Barnabas was led astray.
>
> (Galatians 2:11–13)

If these fanatical Judaizing teachers had succeeded in enforcing their opinions on the Church, demanding circumcision and the observance of the Mosaic Law and Jewish traditions for every Christian, it would most likely have led to two distinct churches. Such a probability was, for Paul, outrageous and required immediate action so as to prevent a continuous rift between Jewish and Gentile Christendom. Boldly and bluntly, he confronted Peter, his fellow apostle, in front of the congregation at Antioch and denounced the attitude that righteousness could be gained through the Law. Should that be possible, then Christ died for nothing (Galatians 2:21). Peter, realizing that he was deviating from the truth of the gospel, was persuaded by Paul's argument. Barnabas and many Jewish Christians were also convinced, but not the Judaizers. This divisive issue needed to be settled once and for all, for the future of the Church was at stake.

The council at Jerusalem (Acts 15:1-35)

The question, How can Jewish Christians eat with Gentile Christians? was a major issue in the apostolic age. This was one reason why the church at Antioch sent a delegation, headed by Paul and Barnabas, to Jerusalem, the mother church, to discuss the matter with the apostles and elders there. The trouble had been caused by men from Jerusalem and so it was logical that the two churches directly involved seek a solution to a problem that would eventually affect Christians everywhere.

Paul had no desire to create a division. He loved all his brothers and sisters in Christ and was therefore deeply concerned about the unity of the Church. No doubt he remembered the mistake he had made prior to his conversion, when such was his intolerance of opposing views that he had persecuted Christians, even to death. Now extreme prejudice and violent hatred were replaced by humility and love. Certainly, he would still vigorously confront error, but would no longer resort to personal abuse. Unrighteous anger should always be avoided because it is indicative of pride and self-interest.

As Paul, Barnabas, and the others traveled to Jerusalem, they visited a number of churches in Phoenicia (modern Lebanon) and Samaria. Noticeably, their conversation was not about the problems at Antioch but rather the fact that Gentiles were being converted. This welcome news made all the believers rejoice (Acts 15:3).

When they arrived in Jerusalem, Paul and Barnabas were welcomed by the whole church and were able to report how God had blessed the Gentiles through their ministry. However, some of the Pharisees who had become Christians declared that all converts must be circumcised and keep the Law of Moses. This obsession regarding the conditions of membership of the

Church for Gentiles, and the stipulations on which Jewish and Gentile Christians could unite, was a vital issue. The outcome of this meeting would affect the future of Christianity worldwide and so it was wise that the leadership of the church in Jerusalem allowed the membership to have their say, no matter how uncomfortable it might have been. Regrettably, in some churches today discussion is occasionally suppressed when dealing with contentious issues because of leaders who are reluctant to listen to those who disagree with them. Pride and a love of power are common major obstacles towards Christians working together.

Instead of continuing the discussion with the general membership, the apostles and church elders met with the delegation from Antioch to consider this serious problem. After a long discussion, Peter, who was well known and respected by the church at Jerusalem, stood up and reminded them that this fundamental question had been settled several years previously in relation to Cornelius and his household (Acts 11:1–18). Then, the incontrovertible evidence had been that God had accepted the Gentiles, for He gave the Holy Spirit to them just as He did to the Jews.

> For there is no difference between Jew and Gentile – the same Lord is Lord of all and richly blesses all who call on him...
>
> (Romans 10:12)

Furthermore, Peter echoes the words of Jesus:

> They tie up heavy loads and put them on men's shoulders, but they themselves are not willing to lift a finger to move them.
>
> (Matthew 23:4)

All Christians have learned to place their heavy burdens upon Jesus (Matthew 11:29). They recognize that both Jews and Gentiles can be justified only through faith in Jesus Christ.

The Scottish theologian William Barclay wrote,

> *Underlying the debate is the difference between a religion of works and a religion of grace. Peace will never come until we realize that we can never put God in our debt, and that all we can do is take what God in his grace gives. The paradox of Christianity is that the way to victory is through surrender; and the way to power is through admitting one's own helplessness.*[1]

When there was no further discussion, everyone listened as Barnabas and Paul told about the miraculous signs and wonders God had done among the Gentiles through them. They did not attempt to embarrass the opposition, for that would have been counterproductive. Rather, they refrained from mentioning circumcision and instead emphasized the recent successes of their mission to the Gentiles. Undoubtedly, God had set his seal of approval upon receiving Gentiles into the Church by faith alone. Miracles of grace are a definite sign of God's favor.

Finally, James, the Lord's half-brother, stood up and acknowledged Peter's contribution. He addressed him by his Hebrew name, Simon (Acts 15:14), which indicates that James identified himself primarily with the Jews. James was a rigorous observer of the Law. Therefore, would he be biased in reaching a decision? Obviously not, for we see that he turns to the Scriptures (Acts 15:16–18, a reference to Amos 9:11–12).

As a result of this, James reaches the admirable conclusion that Gentile converts should not be subject to Jewish regulations, a decision that was readily accepted by the other leaders and the whole church. They disassociated themselves from those who advocated the need for circumcision in order to be saved. The only recommendations within their conciliatory letter to the church at Syrian Antioch were,

> You are to abstain from food sacrificed to idols, from blood, from the meat of strangled animals and from sexual immorality.
>
> (Acts 15:29)

The apostles, the elders, and the church were aware of the presence of the Holy Spirit and the words of the prophets to guide them towards a unanimous agreement that Gentile Christians must not be burdened by needless requirements. Consequently, the council at Jerusalem was a great success in that it ensured unity and fellowship between Jewish and Gentile Christians. Had it failed, it would have led to two churches, neither of which would have served as God's representative.

Reading Acts 15 may give the impression that it is remote from our present situation, even meaningless, because the circumcision party with their Mosaic demands no longer exists. Nothing could be further from the truth, for this passage teaches timeless practical lessons, first in relation to salvation and then to fellowship.

Today there are those who teach that faith in Jesus alone is inadequate for salvation. They emphasize the need for philanthropic works or religious observances so as to be saved. They teach Jesus – plus. That is to falsely say that the work and sacrifice of Christ alone are inadequate for our needs. This is claimed despite the fact that salvation is never a reward for the good things we have done, so no one can boast. Only through the grace of the Lord Jesus Christ are people saved from eternal condemnation.

Peter made the serious mistake of withdrawing from fellowship with professing Christian believers for the reason that they were uncircumcised (Galatians 2:12).

This problem is not so very different from what we see in our churches now. A group thinks that it has all the right answers about church governance, worship practices, and individual behavior and is intolerant of anyone who dares to differ on what are often only secondary issues. For instance, divisions have occurred over different Bible translations. There are the King James group, the New International Version group, the New American Standard group, and other groups. These groups stand firm and some are intolerant of those who use a version different from their own. Such people may be sincere, but they are wrong.

Denominational, racial, and social prejudices should never be a barrier to fellowship. As an example, is it wrong to deny a faithful Christian access to the Lord's table because he or she has not been baptized by immersion or confirmed? Can this be likened to the way Peter refused to eat with the Gentiles?

> Because there is one loaf, we, who are many, are one body, for we all partake of the one loaf.
>
> (1 Corinthians 10:17)

God has accepted people in Christ irrespective of their differences and so must we.

The riches of God's grace

The Judaizers were not the only cause of trouble within the New Testament Church, for at the other extreme there were baptized Gentiles who had lived immorally in their pagan environment. Deplorably, they continued to behave in this manner, believing that the grace of God enabled them to live as they pleased. So, whilst

Acts 15 shows that salvation is not based on a code of religious practice, Jewish or any other, it also underlines a new standard of behavior to be lived out by means of God's power.

Paul had rightly emphasized divine grace as the only source of salvation and so some had wrongly reasoned that there was no point in striving for what is right and just. Also it appeared logical to assume that to continue sinning meant that God could show more and more kindness and forgiveness. As a result, God's grace was turned into a license for immorality, which was a gross distortion of the truth that Paul had taught. Therefore, he makes his position abundantly clear: Christians are no longer slaves to sin but slaves to Christ, and by His power alone, which has overcome sin, they are enabled to defeat temptation.

> What shall we say, then? Shall we go on sinning, so that grace may increase? By no means! We died to sin; how can we live in it any longer? Or don't you know that all of us who were baptized into Christ Jesus were baptized into his death? We were therefore buried with him through baptism into death in order that, just as Christ was raised from the dead through the glory of the Father, we too may live a new life.
>
> (Romans 6:1–4)

The erroneous teaching of the antinomians – that Christians are released from the obligation of observing the moral law – was leading people astray. That is why Paul emphasized the necessity of making a wholehearted break with the sinful life of the past. This was much easier said than done and the church at Corinth is a good example of how some members were reluctant to disassociate themselves from their unenlightened past, thus giving rise to a multitude of problems. These included a spirit of divisiveness, a flagrant case of incest, and members regularly suing each other in the secular law courts. Such attitudes shocked Paul, but rather than walk away from the situation, he made every possible endeavor to restore unity amongst believers.

Paul, writing to the church at Philippi lovingly pleads with two women, Euodia and Syntyche: "Please, because you belong to the Lord, settle your disagreement" (see Philippians 4:2–3; my paraphrase). The cause of the problem is not mentioned. Was it doctrinal, ethical, or personal? We do not know. What primarily concerns Paul is that their dispute had brought division into the fellowship. These two quarreling women had once been enthusiastic and harmonious fellow workers with Paul in the cause of the gospel. They are Christians who need to forgive each other so as to once again work together as a team with one heart and purpose. Such unity will make Paul truly happy.

Although Paul in his letters often stresses the importance of Christian unity, we see that he strongly disagreed with Barnabas as to whether John Mark should join them on their second missionary journey (Acts 15:38). On their previous journey John Mark had shown immaturity by returning home prematurely and so his future commitment was questionable. Obviously, Paul intended to take a man who would prove to be faithful and courageous in times of difficulty. Alternatively, Barnabas believed that John Mark had learned his lesson and should be given a second chance. This was not to be and so Barnabas took John Mark with him and sailed for his homeland of Cyprus. Paul left with Silas, once again commended by the brothers in Antioch, although nothing is said about the trip of Barnabas. Their "sharp disagreement" reveals that they were not infallible or impeccable.

Who was to blame for this unfortunate incident? Probably the fault lies in the failure to consider the various possibilities. Paul could easily have expressed his reservations but agreed to take John Mark, providing that Silas or someone else was also included in the party. This would be an insurance against any subsequent failure by the young man. Whatever the reason, Paul and Barnabas were unable to reach a satisfactory conclusion, though happily Paul was later reconciled to both men (Barnabas: 1 Corinthians 9:6; Mark: Colossians 4:10). Meanwhile, God's providence over-ruled and created two missionary teams, instead of one.

A lust for popularity, position, and power

Self-centeredness is a sin that can lead to conflict with others. This is well illustrated in the Gospels where we see that the disciples sometimes disagree with one another. For example, in Luke 9:46–48 they argue over which of them will be greatest in the Kingdom of Heaven. Evidently, they were more concerned about their own agendas than the Lord Jesus Christ and His will for them.

A similar situation arises in Mark 10:35–45 where Jesus teaches about serving others. (Compare this passage with Matthew 20:20–28.) The attitude of James and John reveals that the desire for personal position and power causes disagreements and divisions. When the other ten disciples learned what had happened they were filled with indignation, thus revealing that their attitude was no better than that of the two brothers. Condemning in others what we excuse in ourselves is a characteristic of human nature in every age.

The true greatness of a person is measured by his or her humility. Jonathan was heir apparent to Israel's throne, but he knew that God would give the kingdom to David. He humbly accepted this fact, for his top priority was loyalty to God. To have a right relationship with God means that there will also be a right relationship with others. Jesus said,

> ... whoever wants to become great among you must be your servant, and whoever wants to be first must be your slave.
>
> (Matthew 20:26–27)

Paradoxically, greatness in God's sight is achieved by a course of action which is opposite to that pursued by an unbelieving world. Godly leadership is about serving others, not personal advancement.

In contrast to this, Diotrophes (3 John 9–11) is a conceited, boastful, and ambitious church leader. He loves to be first and so rejects the apostolic authority of John. Not only that, Diotrophes is a malicious gossip who refuses to welcome the missionaries that John is sending out, or let other members of the church do so. There is no suggestion that the disagreement was because of a theological difference. Rather, the problem probably arose because of Diotrophes' attitude of self-aggrandizement. Such vanity is a primary cause of dissensions and divisions within the Church today.

Beware of false teachers

One of the many problems within the church at Corinth was the presence of false prophets and deceitful workers masquerading as apostles of Christ (see 2 Corinthians 11:1–15). They were preaching a different Jesus, a different spirit, and a different gospel. This was a serious problem within New Testament churches. In Acts 20:29 Paul reminds the Ephesian elders that after he leaves, "savage wolves" will come in among them and "will not spare the flock." Accordingly, they must be permanently vigilant against these heretical teachers and keep a careful watch over themselves and the flock of which the Holy Spirit has made them overseers. Some of these deceivers will arise even from within that congregation (Acts 20:30). This later proved to be true, as we see if we read both letters to Timothy and the risen Christ's letter to the Ephesian church (Revelation 2:2).

Jesus had given warning to watch out for false prophets who "come to you in sheep's clothing, but inwardly... are ferocious wolves" (Matthew 7:15), because they lead people astray. This truth is as relevant now as it was when first spoken, for every generation will encounter its own false prophets. Today many churches have abandoned the Bible and therefore moved away from God. There is "a famine through the land – not a famine of food or a thirst for water, but a famine of hearing the words of the LORD" (Amos 8:11), the consequences of which are disastrous.

There is an urgent need to recognize and refute error whenever it occurs, even though it can be extremely difficult to differentiate between what is true and what is false; the two can be almost indistinguishable because heretics often masquerade as representatives of true Christianity. A gospel that teaches the centrality of Jesus to God's plan of salvation can convincingly be manipulated to meet the ambitions of such leaders. So be on your guard! Where the truth is proclaimed, falsehood is bound to attack.

Right and wrong

Conflict is inevitable in all aspects of human life due to differences of approach and various ideas about what is important. Christians will at times disagree, sometimes vigorously, and this is not necessarily wrong, for it reveals that there is life in the body passionate enough to fight for what is believed to be right. What is totally unacceptable is when people lose sight of the original problem, and sinful human emotions escalate the situation out of proportion. Such unhealthy disagreements are difficult, if not impossible, to resolve and may lead to the tragic division of a church.

The following verse is crucial to a correct understanding of a schism:

> ...there should be no division in the body, but... its parts should have equal concern for each other.
>
> (1 Corinthians 12:25)

All Christians are a part of the Body of Christ upon earth and, as such, a unity should exist between them. It is a sin when selfishness and pride, rather than mutual tolerance and love, lead to dissension and division. This attitude differentiates schism from scriptural separation.

Divisions are sometimes necessary, for if certain people were allowed to stay in a church they would destroy it. Paul makes this abundantly clear to the Corinthian Christian community regarding flagrant sexual immorality. A shocking illicit association had arisen between a man and his stepmother (see 1 Corinthians 5). Even worse was the attitude of the church to the sinner. They were indifferent when they should have been mourning in sorrow and shame. And they had not removed this man from the fellowship.

The action mentioned by Paul to remedy this serious situation was severe and must have caused great consternation for those who heard it. In a dramatic phrase, he says,

> ... hand this man over to Satan ...
>
> (1 Corinthians 5:5)

This should not be interpreted as removing the offender from God and giving him to the devil; it clearly means the immoral brother must be excommunicated. J.B. Phillips helpfully translates this verse:

> The man who has done such a thing should certainly be expelled from your fellowship!

There are many who, in the name of love, reject the need for discipline, but this is a misconception. Discipline when correctly administered is never vindictive or irreversible but is a profound display of Christian love, for its aim is the repentance and reconciliation of the offender. This disciplinary action is also essential for the purity, power, and progress of the Church. Seeking peace through compromise, instead of obedience, will eventually contaminate other members of the Body of Christ, as leaven spreads through bread. Evil is contagious and when a church acts no differently from the world it loses its credibility about what it means to be a Christian. One dysfunctional member can disrupt the whole Body.

Whenever any member persists in denying fundamental doctrine or by sinful conduct brings disgrace on the Church, he or she must be disciplined. According to Scripture, public action is not always necessary or appropriate and excommunication should be a last resort.

> If your brother sins against you, go and show him his fault, just between the two of you. If he listens to you, you have won your brother over. But if he will not listen, take one or two others along, so that "every matter may be established by the testimony of two or three witnesses". If he refuses to listen to them, tell it to the church; and if he refuses to listen even to the church, treat him as you would a pagan or a tax collector.
>
> (Matthew 18:15–17)

When dealing with a difficult problem that cannot be resolved privately, it may be necessary for the leaders of the local church to seek advice. However, the final decision in relation to an unrepentant member must be theirs alone. Also it must be realized that no church is infallible and when mistakes are made they need to be immediately rectified so as to prevent a miscarriage of justice. In such a situation the church leaders, with all the members met together, should apologize to the person concerned, destroy all record of the censure, and rejoice in the restoration of fellowship.

Today's confusion

Today the Church is very different from what it was in the first century. Jesus brought to birth one Church which was to be taken to all nations. Admittedly, even in those early days there was not complete unanimity between believers about what the Church should be like. Even so, their problems were usually satisfactorily resolved and they maintained a united voice during the early centuries.

Regrettably, subsequent history repeatedly reveals occasions when one group broke off from another. A major instance was when serious differences arose between the Eastern (Greek) and Western (Latin) groups, resulting in each faction excommunicating the other in 1054. This is known as the East–West Schism, or the Great Schism. Despite several attempts, the fundamental break has never been healed.

The Western Church became known as the Roman Catholic Church, which, following the Protestant Reformation, itself experienced division, as many people broke away to form new groups. Other divisions were to follow, so that in the twenty-first century there is a multitude of different denominations and groups from which to choose. Many are good, but others teach all kinds of things that are false.

Are you in a church that emphasizes the centrality of Jesus to God's plan of salvation? If not, what should you do?

The ecumenical movement aims to unite all the churches of Christendom, including bringing about the union of Protestantism and Catholicism. Some ecumenists would go even further and advocate the union of all religions. They say, "It does not matter what we believe, as long as we can all be united." That's a lie, for truth must never be sacrificed for the sake of unity. Neither must inter-church cooperation be avoided, providing that this can be accomplished without compromising any fundamental principle. There is no excuse for true gospel churches not working together and proclaiming that all who call on the name of the Lord will be saved.

To think about and discuss

1. Evidently, Peter was not practicing what he believed (see Acts 2:12–13)! Why did Paul react so strongly (Galatians 2:11)? Can you think of similar situations in the Church today?

2. Why is church discipline necessary? How should it be exercised (Matthew 18:15-17)?

3. Why do we not have a united Church on earth today? Who is to blame?

4. Does unity mean that Christians have always to agree?

5. Was the sharp disagreement between Barnabas and Paul wrong (Acts 15:36–41)? Is it possible to say if one or the other was right?

6. Should there be greater cooperation between gospel-believing churches so as to facilitate joint action on matters of common concern? What is the attitude of your own church to working with other denominations and groups?

Notes

1   William Barclay, *Acts of the Apostles* (Saint Andrew Press, 2003), p. 134.

CHAPTER 5

House Meetings and Cell Groups

An encouraging feature of Christianity today is the world-wide proliferation of house meetings and cell groups. This is nothing original, for as we read through the New Testament it becomes obvious that the early believers met regularly inside homes in small groups.

> Day after day, in the temple courts and from house to house, they never stopped teaching and proclaiming the good news that Jesus is the Christ.
>
> (Acts 5:42)

Jason's house at Thessalonica (Acts 17:5) and that of Titius Justus who lived next door to the synagogue at Corinth (Acts 18:7) were used for evangelistic meetings. The early Christians met in homes for the Lord's Supper and shared meals together (Acts 2:46), and also gathered for prayer (Acts 12:12). After Jesus ascended into heaven, the apostles returned to Jerusalem from the Mount of Olives and entered the upstairs room of the house where they were staying (Acts 1:13). Here, with others, they met together primarily for prayer, although subsequent verses indicate that other business matters were also conducted. Later, Paul sent greetings to churches that met in the homes of people such as Priscilla and Aquila (Romans 16:5), Nympha (Colossians 4:15), and Philemon (Philemon 1:2). Initially, house groups or house churches were a crucial factor in the spread of Christianity.

It could reasonably be argued that the early Christians had no church buildings of their own for a long time. They had perforce to use the open air or their homes. They did meet in the synagogues and, no doubt, occasionally hired halls. Paul used the hall of Tyrannus for daily public discussion (Acts 19:9). Often Christians met in the temple courts, usually in the area called Solomon's Colonnade (Acts 3:11; 5:12), for public prayer and praise. This was similar to what Jesus had done. He occasionally taught the crowds in the temple or outdoors, but most often His disciples were instructed in homes (Mark 3:20; 7:17; 9:28, 33; 10:10). Jesus often ministered to people in their homes as He had a meal with them (Matthew 9:10; Luke 7:36). Furthermore, His disciples were encouraged to do the same, and told to wipe the dust off their feet outside any place they were not accepted (Luke 10:5–11). This symbolic gesture was a clear declaration of divine displeasure against anyone who rejected the gospel. By rejecting Christ's message, a man or woman was rejecting Him.

I believe that we need to examine what has happened to the Church since its formation and take a reality check. What did the early Christians do right? What would we be wise to emulate? The evidence suggests that the Church fulfilled the mission of Jesus Christ better when it was decentralized and not unduly organized. The members of the early Church found their homes to be an ideal environment for worship, sharing meals, general conversation, and learning. Does it not appear appropriate that Jesus places emphasis upon the use of homes by describing His followers as a family (Mark 3:31–34)? Surely, it is not an exaggeration to say that small fellowship groups are extremely helpful for Christians to attain spiritual maturity.

The advantages of small groups

In chapter 2 we saw that the early Church faced a problem because the widows of the Grecian Jews were being overlooked in the daily distribution of food (Acts 6:1). As the Church grew, it became more difficult to manage. It is still so. There is always a danger that the larger the Christian fellowship, the less its individual members know, care for, and are accountable to each other. It is very easy to become lost in the crowd, resulting in one's participation being either minimal or that of a spectator. Therefore, it would appear to be advantageous to divide large gatherings into lesser groups such as house meetings or cell groups. This eliminates anonymity, enables mutual accountability, and creates a close community in which everyone can play an active role by developing and fully utilizing their God-given gifts.

But is there not a danger that small groups encourage excessive independence and cause division? I believe that this is unlikely, provided that the leadership spend adequate time training others to lead and give the necessary pastoral support. The aim is to transform passive members into active ministers who are eager to serve. It might also be asked whether or not these extra meetings are likely to become a substitute for the Sunday services. Again the answer is that this is unlikely; in fact my observations suggest that there will be a greater desire to meet on Sundays. Why should that be? Very simply, the more people learn about the value of fellowship, worship, and commitment, the more will be their desire to meet at every opportunity. Usually, a church benefits by meeting regularly both in small groups (cells) and large groups (congregations).

Small groups not only allow people to develop their gifts and experience close personal interaction, but also make it easier for those who are self-conscious or withdrawn to participate. Some seekers of Christ who attend courses such as Alpha or Christianity Explored find, once they have completed the course, that the initial transition to a small house group is less daunting than joining a large church community. Homes should provide a relaxed environment which is conducive to open and honest communication.

By using as many homes as possible, people are enabled to discover the gift of hospitality. It may also enable some people to attend meetings who would otherwise find it difficult, for example, parents who may not be able to find a babysitter, or single people (especially the elderly) who have few opportunities to share their home with others. Hospitality was one of the joys of life in Biblical times and a major factor in the growth of the early Church.

Individualism, leading to a culture of independence and self-sufficiency, is not the will of God either in secular life or in the Christian life. But what is commonly seen today is very distant from what the Bible describes. Some Christians consider fellowship to be no more than meeting together on a Sunday and perhaps for other occasional church events. However, the word for "fellowship" in Greek, *koinonia*, is something much fuller. Its primary meaning is to share in the grace of God. Our fellowship is with God the Father and with His Son, Jesus Christ, and with the Holy Spirit. That is what unites us. But secondly, *koinonia* expresses serious commitment on the part of believers and obligations to each other. True fellowship is what we have, as well as what we receive. In chapter 1 we saw that the early Church enjoyed fellowship.

They devoted themselves ... to the fellowship ...

(Acts 2:42)

This is the first time the term *koinonia* appears in our New Testament.

Traditional churches, especially those that experience rapid numerical growth, can become too large to provide a communal experience. It is a well-known fact that loneliness can be encountered whilst in a crowd, and Christians are not immune to this. There are those who feel a sense of abandonment in a large fellowship and do not know how to share their distress with others. "Small," however, does not necessarily mean "beautiful," for a small group can be as inefficient as a large church. Low numbers are no guarantee of success or increased spirituality. Even so, history repeatedly reveals that the Spirit of God used small groups to achieve phenomenal results. One instance of this is the English Reformation which can be traced back to a few intellectuals who regularly met at the White Horse Inn in Cambridge to study Erasmus' Greek Testament. The Methodist system of societies, classes, and bands, established by John Wesley, provided a source of impetus for the rapid expansion of early Methodism. From modest beginnings, mighty movements have often emerged and spread. As the American poet David Everett commented, "Tall oaks from little acorns grow." Small groups have many advantages, especially a greater sense of fellowship, because all the members know each other.

The "cell" word

Having considered some of the advantages of small groups, we now need to establish the rationale behind the cell structure and how it differs from a traditional house meeting. A casual glance may give the impression that there is little, if any difference, between the two; indeed I believe that if a house meeting is well run, the difference will be negligible. Where cell groups are fundamentally different from most traditional house groups is that they focus outwards and constantly aim to reproduce. This means that if a small group of six or seven eventually grows beyond twelve people, it will divide as a result.

Although cell groups provide a good environment for developing deeper relationships, they cannot guarantee success. It may be found that members of a group are incompatible. Thankfully, the difficulties may be overcome and the group can then progress as a growing unit. However, if a cell functions for a prolonged period without multiplying, it is usually dismantled and the members reassigned to active cells. The aim is that multiplication becomes a recurring feature, thus leading to significant numerical growth. This has resulted in the formation of massive churches in many parts of the world. The most quoted example is that of Dr David Yonggi Cho and his church, the Yoido Full Gospel Central Church in Seoul, South Korea. He began his ministry in the late 1950s with five people and today, it is claimed, the church has about a million members.

It would be a mistake to think that what is applicable in one part of the world will automatically work elsewhere. Care should be taken to appreciate that what works in South Korea is not necessarily repeatable in other cultural settings. Likewise, what suits people in the United States of America may not work in other societies. Effectual basic principles rather than the complexities of methods should always be the prime focus of our attention. It should also be remembered that growth, although important, is only one aspect of what a cell-group church is all about. There is so much more.

Before progressing further, it will be helpful, for the uninitiated, to very briefly consider the historical background. During the time of Mao Tse-tung, the Communists in China developed a cell structure to maintain the social order. Many small groups of citizens would take part in decision making, under the guidance of one or two Party members, so as to ensure that community decisions were compatible with government policy. Christianity was strictly forbidden in Communist China, so the Christians had to meet privately in small groups which became known as "cell churches."

It is reasonable to assume that many of the early New Testament churches were small communities, very similar to cell groups, rather than the traditional churches most frequently encountered today. Was that one reason why early Christianity spread so rapidly? Certainly, the encouraging expansion of Christianity in China, despite severe persecution from the Communist regime, suggests that cell churches are an efficient means of providing spiritual support for their members as well as local community outreach. Similar underground churches also flourished in Eastern Europe under communism and others continue to do so in many parts of the world where Christians are subject to religious intolerance.

The fact that various cell-group churches have achieved amazing numerical and spiritual growth explains the great interest shown by congregations representing a wide range of denominations. Evangelical charismatic groups are especially attracted by this format, although other evangelicals are either implementing or actively considering cell-group church principles.

Are there any weaknesses in the cell-group system? Obviously, such a revolutionary step means that every church member needs to adapt to a change of practice, and this transition period can be difficult, even extremely painful, for some people. Whilst many groups experience remarkable success, others fail miserably. The reasons for this, and how they might be avoided, will be considered later. Doubtless, there are some valuable lessons to be learned about the work of mission, and I am of the opinion that a cell-group structure upholds many key Biblical principles and will undoubtedly play an important role in the future battle for Christianity.

Cell structure

Our physical bodies consist of numerous microscopically small cells which multiply to produce growth. If they cease to function, the body will die. The same principle can be applied to a church. It's no coincidence that Christians are called the "body" of Christ. Paul uses this interesting analogy when writing to the Corinthian church:

> Now you are the body of Christ, and each one of you is a part of it.
>
> (1 Corinthians 12:27)

Every Christian is part of the Body of Christ upon earth and called to do His work. Living cells are active; likewise, a church should be active and reproduce. If it fails, there will inevitably be degeneration, followed by death. Sometimes this may be a slow process, but eventually, if it fails to prod-uce any new life, there's no reason for its existence.

Despite their differences, biological cells usually work together in amazing harmony for the reason that they share a single ingredient: DNA (deoxyribonucleic acid). This material is organized into structures called "chromosomes" that are the carriers of genetic information. Before cells divide, these chromosomes are duplicated in a process called "DNA replication."

Numerous analogies can be drawn between biological cells and an active church cell group. Both are living entities which share a single ingredient. Biological cells contain DNA whereas the power of Jesus resides in Christians. This is what Paul has in mind when he writes,

> ... Christ in you, the hope of glory.
>
> (Colossians 1:27)

Paul worked hard throughout his ministry, but he reminds us of his absolute dependence on God's enabling for the strenuous schedule that he followed and for its effectiveness (Colossians 1:29). This is the means of success for every Christian worker. Christians work, and God works in and through them. All that a church cell group aims to do must be fully focused on Jesus and His teaching. He is the sole source of life, power, and peace.

A body consists of many various parts, but there is an essential unity. Sometimes, however, there are exceptions, and cells become parasites within a body. They share in the benefits but contribute nothing, whereas healthy cells mature and multiply. Similarly, there are people who regularly attend Sunday services and other activities, but in terms of commitment and outreach fail to function in any practical way. They, unfortunately, at best can only be regarded as nominal Christians.

All followers of Jesus Christ should edify one another and also aim to increase the Kingdom of God by regularly sharing their testimony with unbelievers. That is why the cell-group concept takes the Great Commission (Matthew 28:18–20) seriously. However, there is always a great danger that a relentless pressure for quantitative growth degenerates into nothing more than a numbers game. It must be realized that a church is not a machine. To set ambitious growth targets and practice good management is to be commended, but growth should not be confused with mechanistic replication. Hence, care must be taken to ensure that our desire to honor Jesus Christ through evangelism is not substituted by people-focused programs. Otherwise one form of imbalance will be exchanged for another. Only God saves and adds people to His Church (Acts 2:47).

In circumstances where the ultimate aim is for every cell to continuously grow and multiply, there may be a pressure to mass-produce leaders in great haste. As a result, there is an increased risk that spiritually immature people will be placed prematurely into positions of cell leadership. Therefore, careful thought needs to be given to how people are prepared for lay leadership, a vital role that the cell-church vision requires.

The constant need for new leaders is essential if the process of cell multiplication is to continue and gain momentum. So, where do they come from? What are the necessary qualifications? First and foremost, it must be realized that the aim is that the members of a cell are to disciple and exhort each other; to love and care for each other. It is to practice the universal priesthood of all believers (1 Peter 2:5, 9; Revelation 1:5–6). Therefore, it is not primarily theological students who are being sought for cell-group leadership, but those who care for others and can help them to grow through God's Word. Let us remember that God can use the most unlikely people to do His work.

The Lord's anointed

In 1 Samuel 16 we see the limitations of human discernment and the reasons why God chose Jesse's youngest son David to be the future king. On arriving in Bethlehem, Samuel had taken one look at Eliab and thought,

> Surely the LORD's anointed stands here before the LORD.
>
> (1 Samuel 16:6)

But this was not to be.

> ...the LORD said to Samuel, "Do not consider his appearance or
> his height, for I have rejected him. The LORD does not look at
> the things man looks at. Man looks at the outward appearance,
> but the LORD looks at the heart."
>
> (1 Samuel 16:7)

The other sons of Jesse also passed before Samuel, but none
were chosen.

> So he asked Jesse, "Are these all the sons you have?"
> "There is still the youngest," Jesse answered, "but he is tending
> the sheep."
> Samuel said, "Send for him; we will not sit down until he
> arrives."
> So he sent and had him brought in. He was ruddy, with a fine
> appearance and handsome features.
> Then the LORD said, "Rise and anoint him; he is the one."
> ...from that day on the Spirit of the LORD came upon David
> in power.
>
> (1 Samuel 16: 11–13)

Jesus chose disciples who appear to have lacked leadership qualities. Would they be acceptable to most of our
churches? Probably not! Of the Twelve, Judas Iscar-
iot would most likely be considered the best candidate
because of his administrative ability. The first disciples
were fallible people from diverse social backgrounds,
whom Jesus trained for leadership. Their primary qualification for this momentous task was that they personally knew Jesus. They accompanied Him and served their
apprenticeship under His close direction.

The calling of leaders today

How different it is now! The only qualification of some church leaders is an academic degree. Often they lack experience in the secular workplace, something that would tremendously enrich their ministries. Neither have they had the privilege of working alongside experienced Christian leaders so as to learn the art of discipleship. They are strong on theory but weak in practice. I'm not in any way suggesting that intellectual ability is bad. Paul was an outstanding intellectual (Acts 22:3). What deeply concerns me is that many Christians who could effectively proclaim God's Word are overlooked because, like Peter and John, they are considered to be uneducated, ordinary people (Acts 4:13). Is a predominantly middle-class intellectual leadership a reason why the Church today so often fails to reach people from deprived social backgrounds? Is it not necessary to attract leaders from all walks of life?

Active cell groups multiply at regular intervals, which means that the number of leaders must increase accordingly. Therefore, where possible, it is helpful to have an apprentice leader in place at the group's inception. It is always vital not to rush things, as all good leaders take time to develop. Only those who are adequately qualified should be considered for leadership. Today, as always, God insists upon leaders who are people "after his own heart" (1 Samuel 13:14).

It is also essential to be sensitive to the workload that lay people can carry. Therefore, regular ongoing pastoral support is required to prevent a leader becoming isolated or overburdened. The various tiers of leadership that are required to achieve this will depend upon the size and composition of the church. Each must develop the structure that best fits its ministry and ensures effective communication in all directions. Primarily, the pastoral care of the congregation is provided by the congregation itself, whilst the clergy or elders, through delegation, ensure that this happens. This is the most practical and perhaps the only feasible solution within a large fellowship.

Sometimes the cell-church structure, with its many different levels of leadership, can appear to be hierarchical. Thus it needs to be stressed that the demarcation between God's people is that of function, not position. Not every Christian is a leader, but each is a vital part in the spiritual labor of the church.

Cell-group development

Almost every meeting has a form or structure, and cell groups are no exception. So, what should one expect to see in such a meeting? Where does the strategy begin? First and foremost, it should be realized that people are created as relational beings and that when they belong to God, they belong to each other. Jesus said,

> My command is this: Love each other as I have loved you.
>
> (John 15:12)

The majority of church cell groups meet weekly, which is obviously inadequate if meaningful relationships are to develop. The members need to have a closer involvement in each other's lives outside of the regular meeting. Therefore, do they regularly have contact with each other outside of the group? Do they meet together for a meal or other social activity? Do they support each other by providing care in times of need? The success of any group is dependent upon the development of strong relationships, which involves much time and effort.

The regular cell-group meeting is crucial in enabling a passive believer to acquire a sense of participation and purpose. How then can this be achieved? Probably the most commonly adopted format is the so-called four Ws: Welcome, Worship, Word, and Works.

Usually about fifteen minutes would be allowed for the Welcome, fifteen minutes for Worship, one hour for studying the Word, and half an hour for the Works. Putting a time limit on the overall program is usually helpful for some people; those who wish to can always remain after the scheduled meeting is finished.

1. Welcome

Probably the Welcome or "icebreaker" will not appeal to everyone and so some groups will reduce the four Ws to three. However, the evidence suggests that this first element can be a useful means of helping people – especially newcomers or those who are shy – to relax and participate in the meeting from the beginning. Also, over a period of time, a substantial amount of practical information will be revealed about the people in the group, thus enabling closer relationships to develop. The choice of a good icebreaker, namely an activity that allows everyone to contribute, is important and it must be remembered that what works well in one group may be disastrous in another.

Many groups try to relate the icebreaker to the overall theme of the meeting. For instance, on the theme of encouragement, the question may be asked: "How can we find or give encouragement in the midst of problems?" On the theme of happiness: "What makes us happy?" Other groups may begin with a general question such as: "What difficult decisions face people today?"

Whatever topic is chosen, it must be dealt with in a cheerful manner and in no way cause anyone to feel uncomfortable or embarrassed. Remember that it is an icebreaker.

2. Worship

The Welcome is followed by Worship, which allows the group to glorify God in praise and prayer. Notice that this precedes the Word, because seeking guidance by the power of the Holy Spirit is imperative in seeing how the Bible is applicable to everyday life.

3. Word

In studying the Word, the aim is not to talk about the Bible out of mere academic interest, but to put into practice what is learned. James says:

> Do not merely listen to the word, and so deceive yourselves.
> Do what it says. (James 1:22)

Many groups consider the points of the Sunday sermon, and so as to avoid any misunderstanding, group leaders are provided with an outline and the points of application that might be discussed. It is noticeable that Jesus taught primarily through questions and dialogue. He also practiced what He preached. This is the most effective means of communication. People who learn by hearing, asking questions, being shown, and experiencing learn far more than someone listening to a monologue. Within the New Testament there is little evidence for the sermon as we recognize it today. However, it is one of the ways, amongst others, in which the Bible can be taught.

What impact should the Word have on our lives? Certainly, our lifestyle should constantly be a good example to others and proclaim Jesus as Lord. This is a mark of the Spirit's power.

Jesus said,

> ... you will receive power when the Holy Spirit comes on you ...

And then He continued:

> ... you will be my witnesses ... to the ends of the earth.
>
> (Acts 1:8)

Hence, the final part of the meeting is based on Works (perhaps "Witness" would be a more apt title).

4. Works

This is an opportunity for the group to look outwards and consider how to reach those who are not yet Christians. It might involve planning events to which unbelievers can be invited or helping them with some practical need. All these things should be prayerfully considered within the group and, when contacts are established, they should be prayed for specifically, perhaps over a prolonged period of time.

Phil Potter in his excellent book, *The Challenge of Cell Church*, succinctly says, "As the group moves systematically through the four Ws, there's a natural progression – gathering, glorifying, growing and then going."[1] All these stages must be done in the power of the Holy Spirit, otherwise we labor in vain.

To cell or not to cell

Cell-group strategy attracts many accolades today and so, not surprisingly, many churches seriously consider whether or not to adopt such a ministry. Is it the definitive Biblical answer to church growth? Some Christians are of the opinion that cell groups are just another name for a Bible study, prayer meeting, or fellowship group. My position is that the title given to small-group meetings is secondary in comparison to what they do. Undoubtedly, the true cell-group concept practices crucial Biblical principles such as the following:

1. It sees every member in Christ's Body as significant. As a result, everyone can discover and learn how to utilize their God-given gift or gifts.

2. Evangelism is done with a sense of great urgency, as opposed to only talking about it.

3. It strongly emphasizes the need for a meaningful community life and sees the layperson as a potential minister. Members are to take the initiative and care for one another.

All of the above are strategic weapons in the battle for Christianity today. Consequently, this raises the questions: How effective is your church in fulfilling the above criteria? Does your present organizational structure allow for flexibility and diversity? If not, what are you doing about it?

To think about and discuss

1. What reasons can you give to support small-group meetings within a home environment? Are there any disadvantages?

2. What do you understand by the "universal priesthood" of all believers (1 Peter 2:5, 9; Revelation 1:5–6)? Is this practised in your church?

3. How should people be chosen and trained for the responsible position of cell-group leadership?

4. Does introducing more ministries and programs into church life create any problems? Is it sometimes necessary for cells to maintain a sensible "diet" by discontinuing established activities before commencing something new?

5. How can we best demonstrate a commitment to growth, while at the same time avoiding an unhealthy concern with numbers? Does the Bible have anything helpful to say about numbers, counting, and growth?

6. How important is it for a church to have specific targets? What does your church prayerfully plan to achieve within the next five years?

Notes

1   Phil Potter, *The Challenge of Cell Church: Getting to Grips with Cell Church Values* (Bible Reading Fellowship, 2008), p. 38.

CHAPTER 6

Reactions to the Gospel

It is impossible to read the New Testament without realizing that people respond to the good news about Jesus Christ, the Son of God, in extremely different ways. God's Word invariably divides people. So we here ask the questions: What are some of the common reactions of people to their vital need of being reconciled to God? How do they react to Christians and their revolutionary teaching? And why should this be?

Skepticism

Acts 2 vividly describes how the Spirit of God suddenly came upon the believers at Pentecost. Ordinary people were enabled to do extraordinary things because of God's supernatural power. "What does this mean?" the bewildered crowd asked (Acts 2:12). Others, however, ridiculed the apostles and those with them and said they were drunk. Seeing and hearing does not necessarily lead to believing and so some made fun of those who were filled with the Holy Spirit.

Courageously, Peter stood up and addressed the crowd. He assured them that these people were not drunk, as they supposed. It was much too early in the

day for that – even drunkards don't get intoxicated by
nine o'clock in the morning. No, this miraculous occurrence was something predicted centuries before by the
prophet Joel.

Even so, irrespective of fulfilled prophecy, there will
be unbelievers today who object to the advance of Christ's
Church. They ridicule that which is holy and so harden their
hearts to the truth.

Jesus was repeatedly rejected, ridiculed, and abused
because He claimed to be God's only and beloved Son.
Following His arrest, there were people who "spat in
his face and struck him with their fists. Others slapped
him and said, 'Prophesy to us, Christ. Who hit you?'"
(Matthew 26:67–68). According to Mark 14:65 and
Luke 22:64, He was blindfolded whilst subject to the bully-
ing behavior of His assailants. In a group, people usually
behave worse than they do alone and this instance was
no exception. Jesus claimed to be the Christ, possessing
divine power, so now He had the opportunity to prove it
by prophesying who had hit Him. Thus Jesus was repeatedly ridiculed for His apparent weakness.

Shortly before His crucifixion, Jesus was mocked
by the governor's soldiers (Matthew 27:27–31). They
stripped Him and put a scarlet robe on Him. Jesus was
also forced to wear a crown made of long, sharp thorns
and hold a stick in His right hand as a royal scepter.
Kneeling before Him in mockery, the soldiers yelled,
"Hail, king of the Jews!" They were like wild beasts play-
ing with their prey before killing it. Then, when they
became tired of ridiculing Him, they took off the mock
royal robe, gave Him back his own clothes, and led Him
away to be crucified.

Even when He was nailed to the cross, the people
passing by hurled abuse at Him, shaking their heads
in mockery.

"You who are going to destroy the temple and build it in three days, save yourself! Come down from the cross, if you are the Son of God!"

(Matthew 27:40)

They considered it a joke. Jesus had claimed to possess great power and so the people challenged Him to show that by coming down from the cross. It's a horrible picture of the sinful depravity of humankind. "If you are the Son of God" are the same words used by the devil in an attempt to seduce Jesus into sin in the desert (see Matthew 4:3, 6). Now at the cross, a final powerful attempt is made to destroy God's work of redemption, but to no avail. Jesus was crucified because of His abounding love for sinners. He who had the power to calm the raging storm could have lashed out in anger, but He did not. Instead, He who had done no wrong allowed Himself to be led like a lamb to the slaughter.

No servant is greater than his master

Christians who actively proclaim the gospel will also at times be ridiculed and abused. Some are experiencing this now. They are following in the footsteps of their Lord who suffered more than anyone. Therefore, He understands how others suffer, and gives comfort and strength to those who seek Him so that they can follow His example of patient endurance, even to death.

We live in a period of stringent political correctness and it appears that every group has rights, except Christians. No doubt they are considered to be an easy target for ridicule by certain individuals and sections of the mass media. Shouldn't Christians turn the other cheek? Are we not taught to forgive those who sin against us rather than challenge them? While this is true, there are times when Christians have no option but to defend their beliefs and speak out against the blatant blasphemy that so often masquerades as innocuous entertainment or social commentary.

Many thousands of people complained when the British ["Blasphemous"?] Broadcasting Corporation screened *Jerry Springer: The Opera*. This show contained numerous obscenities, unjustly scandalized Christianity, and inevitably lowered the moral tone of the nation. The National Secular Society defended the right to screen the program, urging the BBC not to surrender to "religious bullies." Their vice-president Terry Sanderson said, "This organised attack is the latest attempt by religious interests to control what we can see or say in this country."[1]

Contrary to common belief, the vast majority of Christians are not against freedom of speech. They accept that a wide range of programming is essential for a society consisting of differing ages, backgrounds, and interests. However, if free speech goes beyond the boundary of decency, then Christians must strive in a non-violent manner for the rights that are readily afforded to people in other walks of life.

Physical violence and murder

Perhaps we remember these words we learned as a child: "Sticks and stones may break my bones, but words will never hurt me." Few of us really believe that to be true. Words can be used to hurt and/or heal. Furthermore, the psychological torture caused by ridicule can easily progress to physical violence and murder.

All God's people should expect, at some time, to face persecution. This applies throughout history. When the

Israelites were in Egypt, the Egyptians oppressed them with forced labor and killed their baby sons (see Exodus 1:11–15). Later, the Israelites themselves ignored God's clear commands and persecuted His messengers who warned them of the fatal consequences. The prophet Jeremiah implored God's aid:

> Let my persecutors be put to shame ...
>
> (Jeremiah 17:18)

Many of God's prophets were persecuted.

One might reasonably expect that Jesus during His time on earth would have been admired by everyone. He did many mighty works and healed all kinds of diseases and sicknesses. He preached the good news about the Kingdom of Heaven. His ministry met every human need: emotional, physical, social, and spiritual. Yet, irrespective of this, He was despised, rejected, and then crucified. Why did people turn against Him?

Jesus was considered to be a dangerous misfit by the Jewish establishment and so they convinced the populace to demand His crucifixion. Peter courageously reminded them of this shortly after Pentecost:

> Men of Israel ... You handed him [Jesus] over to be killed, and you disowned him before Pilate, though he had decided to let him go. You disowned the Holy and Righteous One and asked that a murderer be released to you. You killed the author of life ...
>
> (Acts 3:12–15)

Throughout His public ministry, Jesus had been considered by many of the Jewish leaders to have behaved in an irregular and irresponsible manner. They did not like the disreputable people He mixed with and, as a result, He had a reputation of being a friend of sinners (Matthew 11:19). Furthermore, He healed people on the Sabbath, feasted instead of fasted, and even had the audacity of claiming to be equal with God. Surely, this was blasphemy and could not be tolerated.

Jesus launched a scathing attack against the practices of the Pharisees and did not hesitate to expose their hypocrisy. He likened them to "whitewashed tombs, which look beautiful on the outside but on the inside are full of dead men's bones and everything unclean" (Matthew 23:27). These severe accusations were undoubtedly undermining their prestige, which was one major reason for their hostility towards Him. However, Pilate, who was an observant judge of human character "knew it was out of envy that they had handed Jesus over to him" (Matthew 27:18). A gross miscarriage of justice was imminent, for Jesus had to be destroyed before He could jeopardize the status quo.

Jesus said to His followers shortly before His death,

> Remember the words I spoke to you: 'No servant is greater than his master." If they persecuted me, they will persecute you also.
>
> (John 15:20)

He said the same kind of thing to them in Matthew's Gospel:

> All men will hate you because of me…
>
> (Matthew 10:22)

Paul had told the believers that they "must go through many hardships to enter the kingdom of God" (Acts 14:22) and he reminded Timothy that "everyone who wants to live a godly life in Christ Jesus will be persecuted" (2 Timothy 3:12). This is a truth which Scripture repeatedly proclaims.

Those who are in Christ but isolate themselves from the world are not persecuted, for the obvious reason that they have no contact with their prospective persecutors. Likewise, those who are in the world but not in Christ can also live a comfortable life because they are prepared to compromise what the Bible teaches rather than face the foe. In sharp contrast, those who are both in the world and in Christ at the same time will influence society to such a degree that persecution becomes inevitable. Such people, like their Lord, will be social misfits in a sinful world. That is why, following the crucifixion of Jesus, His followers were very soon charged with the crime of proclaiming the gospel message and were persecuted.

Peter and John proclaimed the Word of God boldly and were arrested and imprisoned (see Acts 4). The priests who were present believed that their power and authority were being threatened. They resented the fact that men with no theological training could attract large crowds. Furthermore, Peter in his sermon (Acts 3:12–26) had quoted from the Old Testament to prove to the religious authorities that they had totally missed the point of their own religion. The Messiah had come and they had failed to recognize Him. Even worse, they had crucified the author of life. Naturally, these priests were angry at such accusations. Leaders of religious establishments are often suspicious of and antagonistic towards enthusiastic laypeople because they can so easily disturb the existing state of affairs.

Although the priests were actively involved, it is evident that the major source of opposition was initiated by the Sadducees (Acts 4:1 5:17). These wealthy aristocrats wielded great authority in all aspects of life. Politically, they collaborated with the Romans in order to retain their prestige and most likely were concerned about possible civil unrest if there was no immediate intervention to control the crowd. Public disorder was unacceptable

to the Roman government and any disruption would
have been severely punished. This could have resulted in
disastrous consequences for the privileged status of the
Sadducees. In addition they were extremely annoyed that
Peter and John were claiming on the authority of Jesus
that there is a resurrection of the dead, something which
was contrary to what the Sadducees believed. Christians
will always disturb the peace of those who consider what
Jesus taught to be a rival to their way of life.

Since it was already evening when the apostles were
arrested, they were imprisoned overnight and then the next
day brought before the Sanhedrin, the supreme court of the
Jews (Acts 4:3, 7). The persuasive intervention of Gamaliel
eventually resulted in the apostles being released, but this
was only a temporary lull before the awful storm. It appears
that the early Christians considered that the best form of
defense was attack. As a result, Stephen condemned the
attitude of the Jews who, despite their many privileges, had
consistently persecuted the prophets and then murdered the
Son of God. Stephen's words, to the Jews, were blasphemy,
for which the penalty was stoning to death. Stephen, being
no exception, was stoned by a furious mob and courageously died for his faith. The first great persecution then
broke out against the Church in Jerusalem (Acts 8:1–3).

Today there are many thousands throughout the world
who are harassed, imprisoned, tortured, and killed for being
Christians. Organizations such as Voice of the Martyrs
rightly raise awareness of the current situation and provide much-needed help to those who are oppressed for
their Christian witness. Voice of the Martyrs was founded
through the influence of Richard Wurmbrand; he himself, along with his wife Sabina, was no stranger to horrific
torture under Communist governments. His published
testimony of persecution, *Tortured for Christ*, vividly reveals
how he persevered in suffering for the sake of Jesus.

The mistreatment of believers, or persecution, is not always physical and violent; it can be as subtle as gossip. Paul draws attention to the life the apostles live, and how people curse and tell lies about them. He says they are treated as "the scum of the earth, the refuse of the world" (see 1 Corinthians 4:11–13). This is not to seek pity, but to let the Corinthians know that every true servant of Christ will experience affliction and reproach.

How should Christians respond to persecution? Although the picture appears to be bleak, the Bible also teaches that with the persecutions come blessings.

> ... rejoice that you participate in the sufferings of Christ, so that you may be overjoyed when his glory is revealed.
>
> (1 Peter 4:13)

Instead of looking negatively at our afflictions, Christians must look positively to Jesus and rejoice because of the unconstrained joy that awaits the faithful. In addition, we are to love our enemies and pray for those who persecute us (Matthew 5:44). Our prayer will be that these enemies, by God's grace, will repent and be forgiven.

Wait and see

The vast majority of people today like to remain uncommitted. They dislike being faced with the necessity of making difficult choices. That is why most opinion polls do not insist on a straightforward "yes" or "no" answer but allow for the alternative "don't know." Rather than make a decision, people generally prefer to wait and see what happens.

This is well illustrated when, on their second appearance before the Sanhedrin, the apostles gained an

unlikely ally. Gamaliel, who was a well-respected Phari-
see and the most distinguished rabbi of his day, came to
their rescue when the court seemed likely to resort to
extreme violence.

He addressed his colleagues as follows:

> Men of Israel, consider carefully what you intend to do to
> these men. Some time ago Theudas appeared, claiming to be
> somebody, and about four hundred men rallied to him. He was
> killed, all his followers were dispersed, and it all came to noth-
> ing. After him, Judas the Galilean appeared in the days of the
> census and led a band of people in revolt. He too was killed,
> and all his followers were scattered. Therefore, in the present
> case I advise you: Leave these men alone! Let them go! For if
> their purpose or activity is of human origin, it will fail. But if
> it is from God, you will not be able to stop these men; you will
> only find yourselves fighting against God.
>
> (Acts 5:35–39)

Such an argument appears plausible. However, to say that
if a new movement is of human origin it will fail is not
necessarily true. Certainly, what is from God will ultimately
triumph and what is merely human will eventually fade
away. Also hasty action before the facts are known is foolish.
Nevertheless, in the short term it is not always possible to
judge what is of God and what is not. Evil can be remark-
ably persistent and does not always soon wither away as
Gamaliel suggests.

What was his motive in suggesting caution? There may
have been several reasons, but what is obvious is that he
was not prepared to take sides. There was no commitment
one way or the other. The Sanhedrin accepted his advice to
leave the apostles alone. Then, after having them flogged
and ordering them never again to speak in the name of
Jesus, they let them go. Undoubtedly Gamaliel restrained

the wicked intentions of the council, but is safety what the apostles needed? It is in times of persecution that the Church appears to thrive. The fiery bishop Tertullian (AD c.120–c.220), addressing the leaders of the Roman Empire, boldly declared: "Kill us, torture us, condemn us, grind us to dust … The more you mow us down, the more we grow; the seed is the blood of Christians." The last phrase is traditionally rendered as, "The blood of the martyrs is the seed of the Church." The ability of Christians to face persecution and death, not just with equanimity but with joy, undoubtedly had a mighty impact upon the communities in which they lived.

Courageously, the apostles defied the Sanhedrin's prohibition.

> Day after day, in the temple courts and from house to house, they never stopped teaching and proclaiming the good news that Jesus is the Christ.
>
> (Acts 5:42)

Such a vital message must be proclaimed, whatever the opposition might be. Thus there is a sharp contrast between the Christians and their seemingly reckless courage, and Gamaliel who was over-cautious and much too tolerant. He dodged the issue and probably not for the first time. Where was he when Jesus was being tried before the Sanhedrin? Why didn't he use his influence and intervene to save Jesus?

I must confess that I don't like the attitude of the Gamaliels of this world. They are people who are popular and influential, but indifferent to the truth. There is no commitment to anything positive. Give me the type of people who will take sides, even if they are wrong. When Saul heard about Christianity he was incensed and vigorously tried to destroy it. He was interested enough to take sides. The letter to the church in Laodicea in the book of Revelation reveals that clear-cut support or opposition is better than something in-between. Jesus Christ categorically says that if His followers are not hot (literally "boiling hot"), He would prefer them to be cold (literally "icy cold") – not lukewarm (Revelation 3:15).

One of the major reasons why it is so difficult to promote the gospel is the "let's wait and see what happens" mentality. How long does one wait? What does one expect to see? There are plenty of unsatisfied men and women in the world who, like the superstitious Herod Antipas, would like to see a miracle (Luke 23:8). Even if they did, some would not believe, for often those who had the privilege of seeing God's mighty works viewed them either with indifference or a detached respect.

Now is the day of salvation because yesterday is gone and tomorrow might never come. Hence, it is foolish to wait and see. We read in Matthew 7:13–14 that according to Jesus there are only two gates: one wide, the other narrow. These are entered by two groups, large and small, ending in two destinations: destruction and life. It's "either / or." There is no other way.

God, be merciful to me, for I am a sinner

Peter's first sermon following the outpouring of the Holy Spirit at Pentecost had a great impact upon the crowd. They said to him and to the other apostles,

> Brothers, what shall we do?
>
> (Acts 2:37)

There is no delay in answering this crucial question: all must repent and be baptized in the name of Jesus Christ for the forgiveness of their sins. Then they will receive the gift of the Holy Spirit (Acts 2:38). Baptism in the name of Jesus Christ was and is an outward expression of repentance. It is not a necessity for salvation but a sign of obedience to a sacrament commanded and instituted by the Lord Jesus Christ.

> Those who accepted his message were baptized, and about three thousand were added to their number that day.
>
> (Acts 2:41)

The Bible teaches that there are two types of people in the world: those who are lost and those who are saved. It depends on how they respond to Jesus, who came into the world to save sinners. Those who are lost, as we have already seen, react to the concept of forgiveness either with varying degrees of hostility or with indifference. Because they cling to their own righteousness, they are unable to enter into a close relationship with God. Like those who crucified Jesus, they either wish to destroy Him and His followers, or else shut their eyes and ears to the truth. Thus God's Word is divisive.

Those who do claim to believe in God also react in many different ways. Sadly, some fail to accept the change of lifestyle that following Christ requires and soon give up. Why should this happen? One reason is because there are people professing to be Christians who are not. We find an illustration of this in Acts 8:9–24. A sinister man named Simon, who had been a sorcerer for many years, was amazed at the great miracles and signs performed by Philip the evangelist. If Simon was able to do such things, he would undoubtedly gain power and prestige. He saw many men and women baptized and as a result he too believed and was baptized. He had a professional interest in Philip and followed him wherever he went, no doubt to watch him and see how these miracles were done.

Despite a profession of faith, Simon had not repented of his old life. He still possessed two major traits which should have been absent, namely a boastful attitude (Acts 8:9) and a bargaining attitude (Acts 8:18). He offered the apostles money so as to possess these extraordinary gifts. For this reason, Simon has given rise to the word "simony," meaning the buying or selling of ecclesiastical positions and privileges. Simon made the serious mistake of thinking that you can buy from God those things which He is willing to give. Additionally, he displayed no personal sense of sin, but only a fear of judgment (Acts 8:24). Like many people, from Cain onwards, he was more concerned about his skin than his sin.

Sometimes there are people who follow Jesus Christ because of their own personal agenda. Many Jews initially believed that He was a Zealot liberator who would lead them in rebellion against the Romans. However, when He did not subscribe to their narrow nationalistic views, they quickly turned against Him.

Pseudo-discipleship in our day is a problem. There are people who are attracted to Christianity for the wrong reasons. Some may pretend to be disciples and display all the outward signs of faith. Others are deceived into believing they are disciples by confusing imagination with truth. It is a fact that a large crowd of people can easily be influenced by a common emotion, for example, laughter or sorrow. Therefore, any evangelistic crusade that places undue emphasis upon external factors such as lighting, music, singing, and repetitive phrases is likely to get results. But whenever the theatrical is substituted for the theological, it will ultimately fail. Such responses, however emotional, are a misrepresentation of the work of the Holy Spirit and have no worthwhile spiritual significance. The initial excitement will eventually die and it may lead to the damaging conclusion that Christianity is nothing but a fake.

Contemporary cults often refer to the Bible and may even speak highly of Jesus. As a consequence, they can easily be considered to be representative of authentic Christianity, even though in reality they are antagonistic to its basic doctrines. For many people, they have much to offer. By emphasizing the need for close relationships, they instill a heightened sense of belonging, something which Christianity would also support.

Frequently, cults are based upon some special revelation received by their leadership or some weird interpretation of Scripture that must be rigidly followed. As a result, cults are exclusive groups and it is often claimed that salvation is found in them alone. They can provide convincing answers to the many religious questions with which people regularly struggle. Intellectually, socially, or spiritually, they appear to have much to offer. However, is such faith based on the purpose of God as revealed in the Scriptures? Is Jesus Christ central to God's plan of salvation in the cult's scheme of things?

> ... not by works, so that no-one can boast.
>
> (Ephesians 2:9)

Numerous cults are idolatry masquerading as Christianity, for their worship repudiates the fundamental truths of the Bible.

True disciples, because of their sinful nature, can lose their first love. Their lives can become choked by materialism so that Jesus has little, if any, impact upon them. They may continue to meet regularly at church, or more likely, gradually drift away. When trouble strikes, often in the form of unemployment, illness, or bereavement, there is no anchor to hold them in the storms of life.

At the other extreme are Christians who become so involved in the activities of the church that there is insufficient time to develop a relationship with God. There is no time to read the Bible or to pray, and so they fail to gain a greater understanding of themselves and of God. The risen Christ said to the church in Ephesus:

> Yet I hold this against you: You have forsaken your first love.
>
> (Revelation 2:4)

Can we truthfully say that we are as much in love with the Lord today as when we first knew Him?

A casual glance at the Ephesian Christian community appears to set an example that should be followed. Most of us would be delighted to worship with such a large fellowship. Its members were active, patient in their sufferings, and would not tolerate false doctrines. Yet despite all this, they had somehow forsaken their love for Christ. A passion for truth without love is a dangerous thing, for it develops into either religious formalism or fanaticism.

How is lost love to be recovered? The answer to the church in Ephesus is to remember the height from which they have fallen, and to repent and return. God is always faithful to forgive those who confess their sins. If they do not return, their ministry will be terminated for, without love, the Church has no light. Ephesus was one of the greatest churches of its day and if it must take care lest it should fall, so must we. Let us pay careful attention to this warning before it is too late.

Satan will always try to discredit God's work. If Christians cannot be restrained, so he reasons, then they must be driven to extremes of excitement and emotion. Formalism will be replaced by fanaticism so as to cause division and distress. Christians must constantly be careful that their own feelings are not misrepresenting the work of the Holy Spirit. To do so introduces practices or beliefs which are based on imagination instead of God's revelation. As a result, there are many "ultras" and extremists who cause confusion by creating unbiblical splinter groups. One such group is the extreme Calvinists (or hyper-Calvinists) who believe in the sovereignty of God to such a degree that they completely ignore the free will of humankind. "Evangelism is not necessary," they say. "If God wants to save someone, He will do so."

In the 1700s William Carey, a cobbler by trade, became burdened for a definite missionary outreach. When he shared his burden at a meeting of Baptist ministers, he was told by a senior minister: "Young man, sit down!" The older man then added: "When God wants to convert the heathen, He will do it without your help or mine." Thankfully, Carey did not let his enthusiasm be dampened by such a negative response, and eventually answered all the usual arguments against missions, showing that the Great Commission to evangelize was not only for the original disciples but applicable to every generation. True, God is sovereign over everything.

> The LORD does whatever pleases him,
>> in the heavens and on the earth,
>> in the seas and all their depths.
>
> (Psalm 135:6)

Even so, this in no way negates human responsibility which includes going and making disciples of all nations.

Jesus tells us that some people are fruitful.

> ... the one who received the seed that fell on good soil is the man who hears the word and understands it. He produces a crop, yielding a hundred, sixty or thirty times what was sown.
>
> (Matthew 13:23)

It is noticeable that there is a marked difference in the yield. Not all are equally productive in bringing others to Christ.

Each, however, loves Jesus Christ and readily shares that love with others.

Two people may pray and preach with equal zeal and faithfulness, and yet get very different results. An individual may see their labors bear more fruit at certain times and not others. For example, on his second visit to America in 1740, George Whitefield was mightily used by God in the Great Awakening. However, during subsequent visits, he never witnessed such a great harvest again. Numerous others who have faithfully labored for the gospel would acknowledge that at certain times they saw far more conversions than they did at other times. The common idea that prayerful evangelistic activity invariably leads to a great harvest of souls is disproved by facts. Why should this be? The answer lies with God Himself. Paul says,

> I planted the seed, Apollos watered it, but God made it grow. So neither he who plants nor he who waters is anything, but only God who makes things grow.
>
> (1 Corinthians 3:6–7)

Christians do the fieldwork in preparation for growth, like sowing, planting, watering, and weeding. But then their activity stops, for only God can make the plants grow and give the increase. Thus God must receive the entire honor and all the glory.

It is noteworthy that today great emphasis is placed upon revivals and outpourings of the Holy Spirit as are described in the book of Acts. Certainly, from time to time the Holy Spirit falls in exceptional power, bringing new life to the Church and salvation to many souls. Such a revival leaves a permanent mark. Sometimes, however, "revival" is used to describe a specific evangelistic effort. This, I believe, is misleading for it confuses "evangelism," which involves a man or woman serving God, with "revival," which is the sovereign work of God on behalf of people.

When the Spirit came down at Pentecost, the people were "amazed and perplexed" (Acts 2:12). God never ceases to amaze, for His ways are far beyond anything we can imagine. Therefore, although fervent prayer frequently precedes revival, there are no fixed rules. God blesses whom He wants, where He wants, when He wants. God is sovereign and not bounded or limited by the dictates of others or by the circumstances of time.

Paul, looking back over his long ministry says,

> I have fought the good fight, I have finished the race, I have kept the faith.   (2 Timothy 4:7)

Several years previously, speaking to the elders of the Ephesian church, Paul had indicated his desire to achieve this:

> ... I consider my life worth nothing to me, if only I may finish the race and complete the task the Lord Jesus has given me – the task of testifying to the gospel of God's grace.
> (Acts 20:24)

Now he can say, "I have finished the race." He has also kept the faith by guarding the gospel message with his life, to prevent it being diluted or distorted.

Whenever the truth is proclaimed, falsehood is certain to attack. Hence, Christians today, like Paul, have a fight to be fought, a race to be run, and a gospel to be faithfully proclaimed. Each involves strenuous work, great sacrifice, and even great danger, but these momentary troubles are nothing compared with the blessings to come.

These words spoken by Jesus should be etched in the mind of every Christian:

If you then, though you are evil, know how to give good gifts to your children, how much more will your Father in heaven give the Holy Spirit to those who ask him!

(Luke 11:13)

Therefore, our prayer must be that the flame of the Holy Spirit will ignite our lives so that we have the courage and strength to witness whenever and wherever necessary. If God is for us, it matters not who is against us. The unmistakable message of the Bible is that Jesus wins, and those who suffer with Him will one day share His glory. Thus we can look to the future with confidence because of our security in Christ. Meanwhile, let us strive to love and honor God in all we do by worshipping Him in Spirit and truth.

To think about and discuss

1. Why do people respond to the gospel in diverse ways?
2. Discuss the various strategies used by Satan to lead people astray.
3. Do you agree with the claim in this chapter that the advice of Gamaliel is not a satisfactory principle to follow in discovering the will of God?
4. What different reactions to the gospel have you experienced? How well do these match the different kinds mentioned in this chapter?
5. How can one differentiate between true Christianity and that which is false?
6. Paul said,

   I have fought the good fight, I have finished the race, I have kept the faith. (2 Timothy 4:7)

   How should we go about this? (See Ephesians 6:10–20.)

Notes

1 Quoted in Ciar Byrne, "BBC to show 'Jerry Springer – The Opera' despite a record chorus of complaints", *The Independent* (8 January 2005). This article can be viewed on the Web.

About the Author

Christopher Brearley served as an elder at St John's Wood Road Baptist Church, London for almost twenty years before retiring to York in March 2004. He has been preaching and teaching since 1976 and has travelled extensively both at home and abroad. He continues to be actively involved in an itinerant ministry and writing. His 2007 book, *Does God Approve of War?* was also published by Sovereign World.

Also available by the same author

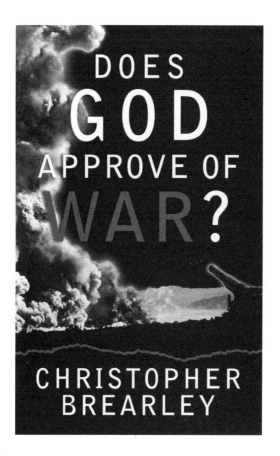

Does God Approve of War?

Christopher Brearley

The author draws upon many examples from history to illustrate a variety of arguments that either defend the action of war or oppose it. Insights into war are derived from both the Old and New Testament - how do these historical events help us today to understand whether war can be justified in modern society. This book will help the reader approach this question critically and scripturally.

£5.99 / 96pp / 9781852404666 / www.sovereignworld.com

We hope you enjoyed reading this
Sovereign World book.
For more details of other Sovereign
books and new releases see our website:

www.sovereignworld.com

You can also join us on Facebook and Twitter.

If you would like to help us send a copy of
this book and many other titles to needy
pastors in developing countries, please
write for further information or send your
gift to:

Sovereign World Trust
PO Box 777
Tonbridge, Kent TN11 0ZS
United Kingdom

www.sovereignworldtrust.com

The Sovereign World Trust
is a registered charity.